DEVELOPMENTS IN THE EARLY RENAISSANCE

Contributors

John Charles Nelson
Columbia University

Lynn White, jr.
University of California, Los Angeles

Rudolf Wittkower
Late of Columbia University

Joseph R. Strayer
Princeton University

Paul Oskar Kristeller
Columbia University

Richard McKeon
The University of Chicago

Developments in the Early Renaissance

Papers of the second annual conference
of the Center for Medieval and
Early Renaissance Studies
State University of New York at Binghamton
4-5 May 1968

Edited by Bernard S. Levy

STATE UNIVERSITY OF NEW YORK PRESS
ALBANY

Published by State University of New York Press
Thurlow Terrace, Albany, New York 12201

© 1972 by State University of New York

Library of Congress Cataloging in Publication Data

Developments in the Early Renaissance.
Edited by Bernard S. Levy.
"Papers of the second annual conference of the
Center for Medieval and Early Renaissance Studies,
State University of New York at Binghamton, 4–5 May 1968."
Includes bibliographies.
1. Renaissance—Congresses. I. Levy,
Bernard S., 1927– ed. II. New York (State).
State University at Binghamton.
Center for Medieval and Early Renaissance Studies.
CB361.D46 914'.03'21 77–129641
ISBN 0–87395–076–3
ISBN 0–87395–176–X (microfiche)

Contents

Preface
7

The Poetry of Michelangelo
JOHN CHARLES NELSON
15

The Flavor of Early Renaissance Technology
LYNN WHITE, JR.
36

Hieroglyphics in the Early Renaissance
RUDOLF WITTKOWER
58

The Origins of the Early Modern State
JOSEPH R. STRAYER
98

The Impact of Early Italian Humanism
on Thought and Learning
PAUL OSKAR KRISTELLER
120

The Transformation of the Liberal Arts in the Renaissance
RICHARD MCKEON
158

Preface

The six essays contained in the present volume were originally read at the second annual conference sponsored by the Center for Medieval and Early Renaissance Studies of the State University of New York at Binghamton. Where necessary the papers have been revised to fit the format of an essay rather than of the lecture originally presented. Since the vastness of the general subject, "Developments in the Early Renaissance," precluded the possibility of including even a selective bibliography for so rich a field, it seemed the better part of wisdom to allow each participant to offer a bibliography and notes suitable to his own contribution. For much of the value of this book will be found in the individual essay, where each author has the opportunity to explore an important aspect of this varied field, often providing a general introduction to a rather limited topic, where even a minute detail can serve to illuminate the subject. The book thus offers something of interest for both the specialist and the general student of the Renaissance; for though the conference could not attempt to encompass every field of importance for the early Renaissance, the papers do, in their frequently wide-ranging allusions, present an invaluable introduction to what might be called, to borrow a phrase from Professor White, the flavor of the early Renaissance; and success at such an endeavor is no mean achievement.

Despite the effort of the conference to achieve breadth, the papers do have something of their own coherence as a collection, for each deals in its own way with the spirit of innovation that we have come especially to associate with the early Renaissance, the first three on a relatively narrow and the final three on a much wider scale. While the first three focus on fairly limited but quite different topics, yet each is specially concerned with the creative individualism that is so important to those developments in the early Renaissance which give the period much of its special flavor.

Professor John C. Nelson was kind enough to substitute at the last moment for Professor Nathan Edelman, since the latter was unable to attend the conference because of illness. Professor Nelson's paper on "The Poetry of Michelangelo" was first read as one of a series of lectures on various aspects of Michelangelo's work, at Columbia University during November 1964, in commemoration of the four hundredth anniversary of his death. Although Michelangelo may perhaps be considered as representative of a period somewhat later than what we might call the early Renaissance, his poetry does reflect the conventions of the earlier period, and the importance of such an influence is central to Professor Nelson's interest in Michelangelo's poetry. For in the Renaissance, as Professor Nelson suggests, the blending in love poetry of the Christian with the Platonic and the spiritual with the sensual can sometimes lead to disagreement as to whether the motive behind a given poem is mainly physical or mainly spiritual. Focusing on a limited number of Michelangelo's sonnets, Professor Nelson examines the background of Michelangelo's poetry and discusses the relationship between the Platonic, Petrarchan, and Christian influences that affect the poetry in order to explore the much-vexed question of the degree of their emphasis on the sensual and the relevance of such an analysis to Michelangelo's personal life, an analysis that reveals the sort of individualism that we have come to associate with the Renaissance.

We may have come to expect the Renaissance to reveal such individualism in its poetry and in the personal life of an important artist, but such creativity proves rather unexpectedly to play an important role in so seemingly practical a field as that of technology. The early Renaissance was a period of rapidly advancing technology, but technology did not advance then, as it is often assumed that it did today, by the practical application of scientific discovery. Rather, as Professor Lynn White, jr., demonstrates in his essay, "The Flavor of Early Renaissance Technology," technology advanced then, "not by the application of scientific discovery," but "by supplying the instrumental needs of science." By further explorations of their contributions he also proves that engineers of the early Renaissance show evidence of a creativity that transcends the practical. Though such a quality may not be considered usual in the realm of technology, it is a quality that we associate with men of the fifteenth and sixteenth centuries. It is only by understanding this innovative quality of engineers "who seem most often to be indulging in a speculative empiricism which is almost playful in character," Professor White argues, that we can appreciate the spirit of early Renaissance technology and of men who as a result made important contributions to later technology.

Playfulness may seem unusual in the realm of technology, but it comes as no surprise in art. Professor Wittkower focuses on what may at first seem merely a playful aspect of Renaissance art but proves in fact to reflect some of its most important philosophical concerns. Despite its demonstrated importance, most general studies of the period fail to consider the significance of hieroglyphics in the Renaissance. In his essay, "Hieroglyphics in the Early Renaissance," Professor Rudolf Wittkower focuses his attention on the Neoplatonic concepts and the influential though, from the twentieth-century point of view, mistaken interpretation of hieroglyphics which combined in the Renaissance to give hieroglyphics and derivative pictorial symbols expression in various art forms. It was believed that "Plato and pre-Christian revelations attested to the truth of Christianity by way of veiled mysteries" and that hieroglyphics were pictorial images that embodied the essence of an idea that could be grasped only intuitively. Creative artists therefore used pictorial symbols, but they directed them to an elect few capable of an immediate apprehension of such mysteries. Professor Wittkower presents many examples to illustrate and support his argument that the Renaissance understanding of hieroglyphics and the prevalent desire to reconcile Christian and pre-Christian mysteries brought about a merging of hieroglyphics with Renaissance allegory and symbolism which is reflected in its art.

While these three papers focus on what may seem at first sight somewhat limited aspects of the early Renaissance and yet offer insight into its creative flavor, the final three papers are concerned with another important feature of the early Renaissance: the development of innovations on a larger scale which prove to be of central importance to later centuries.

Professor Strayer traces the development of the local medieval European political community into the large modern state. It was, as he shows, a long and gradual process, requiring several centuries, and the early modern state inherited both the strengths and the weaknesses of the medieval institutions. Those medieval institutions concerned with internal affairs were the first to develop fully. Consequently, a crisis arose when it became necessary for rulers to deal with external foreign affairs for which no institutions had evolved. Professor Joseph R. Strayer concerns himself with this crisis, and the ways in which it was met, in his essay, "The Origins of the Early Modern State." As he shows, the crisis required the development of a new bureaucracy, which emerged from the policy-making body, the Council, composed of men more amenable to the wishes of the ruler than the old bureaucrats and better equipped to deal with the problems of the modern world. The increasing importance of the Council also led, as Professor Strayer shows, to the creation of a new bureaucracy with special departments, and the nature of the division of functions and of the amount of power granted to the Council and its departments affected the future structure of most European states.

Developments in the early Renaissance were important not only in the political but also in the intellectual realm. As Professor Kristeller vigorously argues, humanism was of great importance to the cultural and intellectual climate of the Renaissance, and it contributed much to the thought and learning of later centuries. The nature of the achievement and the extent of the contribution of the early Italian humanists to subsequent intellectial development is the central concern of Professor Paul Oskar Kristeller in his essay, "The Impact of Early Italian Humanism on Thought and Learning." Professor Kristeller interprets Renaissance humanism as "the intellectual movement associated with the rise and expansion of the humanities" and treats early humanism as the period from 1280 to 1500. Because he believes that the contribution of the Italian humanists to classical learning has been greatly underestimated, he provides a broad survey of his subject from three different perspectives: the achievement of Italian humanism within the domain of the humanities, its diffusion outside of Italy, and its impact on other fields of learning. Such a survey enables him to conclude that "early Italian humanism was an important and influential movement that had a great and pervasive impact on the thought and learning of its own time and of subsequent centuries."

Professor McKeon also deals with the intellectual climate of the period, but he focuses on the transformation of the liberal arts which began in the early Renaissance in order to offer us a perspective from which we can judge the Renaissance objectively. It is extremely difficult for the historian to achieve an impersonal interpretation of history, and especially of the history of culture; and often misconceptions handed down from an earlier time hinder the pursuit of such objectivity. Since our views of the Renaissance have been greatly influenced by nineteenth-century interpretation — in his essay, "The Transformation of the Liberal Arts in the Renaissance," Professor Richard McKeon suggests a history of the liberal arts can contribute to an understanding of the present interpretation of the liberal arts which can lead to a more impartial appraisal, for it will allow us to correct the current view of the Renaissance in the light of the current conception of the liberal arts. An understanding of the liberal arts is important to such an undertaking, Professor McKeon argues, because they themselves are the means by which the culture of an era is interpreted and understood. They also provide an objective basis for making distinctions which would otherwise remain subjective, for the liberal arts allow the historian of culture to take into account his own perspective. Professor McKeon traces the history of the liberal arts from the Middle Ages, when the liberal arts were conceived of as "universal *disciplines*," through the Renaissance, when they were considered to be "particular *subject matters*," to the present time, in which we are still engaged in our own transformation of the liberal arts. And he follows the development of four different aspects which reveal the changes which took place in the conceptions of the liberal arts. Only such an analysis, Professor McKeon suggests, will lead us to an impartial appraisal of the Renaissance. Professor McKeon's essay thus provides a fitting conclusion to the collection. It not only offers insight into the early Renaissance through its analysis of its transformation of the liberal arts, but it also presents the enticing possibility of an objective reinterpretation of the Renaissance as a whole.

BERNARD S. LEVY

The Poetry of Michelangelo

Much can be learned about Michelangelo's poetry from the analysis of even a single representative poem. Let us consider, for example, the following sonnet, chosen from his 302 extant poems, and translated as literally as possible.

> Non so se s'è la desïata luce
> del suo primo fattor, che l'alma sente,
> o se dalla memoria della gente
> alcun' altra beltà nel cor traluce;
>   o se fama o se sogno alcun produce
> agli occhi manifesto, al cor presente,
> di sé lasciando un non so che cocente
> ch' è forse or quel c' a pianger mi conduce.
>   Quel ch' i' sento e ch' i' cerco e chi mi guidi
> meco non è; né so ben veder dove
> trovar mel possa, e par c' altri mel mostri.
>   Questo, signor, m' avvien, po' ch' i' vi vidi,
> c' un dolce amaro, un sì e no mi muove:
> certo saranno stati gli occhi vostri.[1]

I do not know whether my soul feels the longed-for light of its Maker [that is, the light to which it wishes to return], or whether

15

some other source of beauty seen among people, remaining in memory, now shines in my heart, or whether fame or dreams give back to me the image of someone manifest to my eyes and present in my heart, leaving an unspecifiable ardor which is, perhaps, what leads me now to weep. Neither that which I feel and see nor he who might guide me is with me; nor can I see where to find my goal, though it seems that someone is showing me the way. This has happened to me, my lord, since the day I first saw you. I am moved by bittersweetness, by yes and no: certainly the fault belongs to your eyes.

In many of Michelangelo's poems we find images so striking that we feel at once that they are spontaneous expressions of the poet's feeling, deriving, as the case may be, from a cherished recollection of things seen; from the sculptor's meditation; from wry reflection on life's paradoxes. But there are even more poems, where, if we look for the mark of originality or spontaneity, we will either find it lacking, or, as in the sonnet we have just read, find that it consists in Michelangelo's manner of juxtaposing and rethinking elements of the poetic tradition inherited by all cinquecento poets. While Dantean and Bernesque flashes appear throughout his *Rime,* it comes as no surprise to find Petrarchism and Platonism woven strand-by-strand through the majority of his poems.

Let us identify these elements in the poem we have just read. In the opening quatrain, the soul's desire to return to the light of its Maker has strongly Platonic overtones. The return journey of the soul to its patron god or its parent star, retracing in the upward path of love and knowledge the downward thrust of divine creation, was a frequent theme of prose theorists and poets following Marsilio Ficino's monumental translations and interpretations of the complete works of Plato and Plotinus in the latter' part of the fifteenth century. Generally this theme and others taken over from Plato were couched in Christian, or at least nonpagan, terms. The less philosophically oriented Platonizing writers, among whom we should include Michelangelo, easily blend Platonic and Christian spirituality without even noticing the points of conflict that troubled Girolamo Benivieni and the proverbially erudite Giovanni Pico della Mirandola and which were to spell trouble a century later for the professional philosophers, Francesco Patrizi and Giordano Bruno.

Now, one might disagree with our labeling as specifically Platonic the opening thought of this sonnet — the soul's desire for the light of its Maker. One might observe that if there had never been a Platonic revival in Florence in the fifteenth century, continuing until well after Michelangelo's death, the idea of the soul's return to the Divinity, as Christian as it is Platonic, here coupled with the metaphor of light, might well have reached Michelangelo through Dante's *Paradiso*. Certainly it is the case with Michelangelo, as it is with almost every other important Italian Renaissance poet, that Dantean and *stil-nuovo* motives, often themselves ultimately of Neoplatonic derivation, are inseparably intermingled with elements of the later Platonic revival initiated by Petrarch and carried to fruition by Ficino. The second idea of this sonnet, beauty as a memory cherished in the heart, might convince us, associated as it is with the first idea, of their common Platonic inspiration. We must observe that the memory is not Socrates' reminiscence of an eternal essence glimpsed in the soul's previous life in the empyrean, but the memory of a human face or form seen in the society of men. Even so, it is just the sight of such beauty that starts the soul on the restless search which Michelangelo describes in the remainder of this sonnet and which Plato details in the *Phaedrus*. Yet here, also, the motive of remembered beauty shining in the lover's heart could be a reflection of *Rime* written by Dante and other poets of the *dolce stil nuovo*. Again, we are faced with a multiple derivation.

In the second quatrain the irrepressible sensuality expressed by the words "un non so che cocente" is too forceful to be restrained by the bonds of Platonism as interpreted by the Italian Renaissance. The struggle of flesh against spirit, the hallmark of Petrarch's poetry, familiar to all Christians from personal experience if not from Augustine's *Confessions*, asserts itself.

In the first tercet (ll. 9-11), the author feels that disoriented, restless dissatisfaction which, according to the Platonic Socrates and his later disciples, characterizes all earthbound loves. In the concluding tercet the ascent to the higher world envisioned by the Platonists fails to occur, though it does in some other sonnets by Michelangelo, and the poet is left in that state of bittersweet reverie made so familiar to everyone by Petrarch.

In the following sonnet the Platonism is even more unmistakable:

> Veggio nel tuo bel viso, signor mio,
> quel che narrar mal puossi in questa vita:
> l'anima, della carne ancor vestita,
> con esso è già più volte ascesa a Dio.
>   E se 'l vulgo malvagio, isciocco e rio,
> di quel che sente, altrui segna e addita,
> non è l'intensa voglia men gradita,

l'amor, la fede e l'onesto desio.

    A quel pietoso fonte, onde siàn tutti,
s'assembra ogni beltà che qua si vede
più c'altra cosa alle persone accorte;
    né altro saggio abbiàn né altri frutti
del cielo in terra; e chi v'ama con fede
trascende a Dio e fa dolce la morte.

                            [*Rime, 83*]

I see in your handsome visage, my lord, something which is hard to imagine in this earthly life: your soul, still united with your flesh, has already several times, with your visage, made the ascent to God. And if the vicious crowd, foolish and guilty, attributes to others its own ignoble sentiments, yet not even so are my intense craving, my love and faith and honorable desire, any less dear to me. Every beautiful thing which is seen on earth, in the judgment of the wise resembles more than any other thing that divine fount from which we all derive; nor do we have on earth any other example or other fruits of heaven; and he who loves you faithfully rises up to God and thinks death sweet.

Here we see at once the Platonic scheme of two worlds — the essential and divine realm above us and the shadowy corporeal world around us — where man must reject what is vicious and merely material in order to see and experience the beauty which can lead the soul in Diotiman ascent to the source of all beauty, triumphant over death and evil and the flesh.

The derivation of Michelangelo's Platonism is as easy to explain in a general way as it is difficult to pinpoint in specific detail. According to an anonymous, unpublished, Renaissance biographer of Girolamo Benivieni, quoted by Giovanni Papini in his *Life of Michelangelo*, Benivieni predicted a brilliant future for the artist, such as to retain for Florence her primacy in art, when Michelangelo was a thirteen-year-old novice in the workshop of Ghirlandaio.[2] Incredible? Perhaps. But it is certain that Michelangelo, at fifteen, was received by Lorenzo il Magnifico into the Medici household, perhaps as a result of Benivieni's praise. In the palace on the Via Larga Michelangelo inevitably came under the influence of other Platonizing humanists and poets — Marsilio Ficino, Angelo Poliziano, Giovanni Pico della Mirandola, and others who either were members of the Medici circle or who were frequent visitors to Lorenzo. The Platonic coloration of his poetry can be explained by this fact alone.

Thus it comes as no surprise to us that Michelangelo, who knew everyone in the Medici circle in his youth, whose character was deeply spiritual, and who read the poetry of other contemporary Petrarchizing and Platonizing poets, should employ Neoplatonic motives in his poems, now clearly, now vaguely. This does not mean that we can put our finger on a line of his poetry and say, "This concept was taken from Marsilio Ficino," but we can affirm that his poetry is imbued with a Platonic spirit. Indeed, if there is one characteristic of Michelangelo's Platonism which distinguishes it from that of other poets of his time, it is his unmistakable sincerity. For Michelangelo Buonarroti, Platonism was not lip service to a current literary fashion as it was for so many of his contemporaries — such as Lorenzo, Bembo, and Castiglione, to name three; it was the expression of a deeply felt affinity for spiritual concerns. The same genuineness characterizes his somber religious sonnets to Vittoria Colonna. Even his *scherzi* in the manner of Burchiello and Berni bear the imprint of his strong personality — the hallmark, ultimately, of all his poetry —

which sets him apart from the many lesser poets of his age whose literary preparation far exceeded his own.

Let us return to the first sonnet that we read, "Non so se s'è la desïata luce." It was written and rewritten several times by Michelangelo. The autographs are still extant. Two of the redactions are translated by John Addington Symonds; the second of these is the one which we have read. In the earlier draft Michelangelo employed, in line 12, the word *donna* ("lady") instead of *signore*. It appears from the several texts collated by Enzo Girardi (*Rime*, pp. 237-43) that Michelangelo originally composed this sonnet for a lady, and then decided to send it to his friend Tommaso Cavalieri.

Symonds's translation of the concluding tercet of the earlier redaction, to the lady, reads as follows:

> This, since I saw thee, lady, makes me weak:
> a bitter-sweet sways here and there my mind;
> and sure I am thine eyes this mischief breed.[3]

It is no accident that his translation of the same lines in the later redaction, where the word *signore* is used instead of *donna*, is identical (that is, even the word *signore* is translated "lady" instead of "lord"). It was Cesare Guasti's opinion, when he published the first critical edition of Michelangelo's *Rime* (Florence, 1863) that Michelangelo had intended for the poetess Vittoria Colonna the poems which we now know were written to Cavalieri. Much earlier, in 1623, the artist's grand-nephew, Michelangelo Buonarroti the younger, in the earliest edition of the *Rime*, had purposely altered a few of his granduncle's expressions, changing some masculine words to their feminine counterparts.

Later editors and interpreters of Michelangelo's *Rime* were reluctant to believe that some of his finest poems had been inspired by a handsome young Roman nobleman; yet Benedetto Varchi, a prominent cinquecento man of letters, had stated in a public lecture apropos of a certain sonnet by Michelangelo, without the slightest suspicion of scandal: "[This sonnet is] addressed to Messer Tommaso Cavalieri, a most noble Roman youth, in whom I found, when I met him in Rome, besides his incomparable beauty of body, such charming behavior, such excellent intelligence and gracious ways that he indeed deserved, as he still does, that the better one knew him, the more one loved him."[4]

There is, however, another possible reason for the later reluctance to see what Varchi saw and accepted. In early Tuscan poetry, as before it in Provençal poetry, masculine designations such as "lord" instead of their feminine counterparts were employed in poems written to ladies. The reason for this strange custom is not hard to find: it is well known that with the sudden appearance of the poetry of courtly love in Southern France around the year 1100 and its novel, not to say revolutionary, way of celebrating women as objects of romantic love, the lady was placed upon a pedestal, giving her the same position of command over her lover as the feudal lord exercised over his vassal. Hence she was his lord and could be so addressed.

There also remained, from the Platonic dialogues, translated by Ficino, the male-oriented picture of love which Plato had painted. Love in these dialogues, however lofty its ultimate goal, begins as the love of two men (generally a mature man and a younger man) for each other. In their interpretations of Platonic myth and doctrine, the Renaissance Platonist philosophers employed abstract terms such as "beloved" and "object of love" which avoided reference to the sex of the persons involved, or else attributed to the lovers only a moral and intellectual fervor. Giuseppe Betussi said of love between two persons of the same sex, "It can be true and most perfect while it is concerned with the beauties of the soul and it is licit; just as it becomes illicit when it tends toward another end."[5] To Marsilio Ficino, who first used the term "Platonic love," the words signified an intellectual love between friends based on the individual's love of God. Such relationships, as Professor Kristeller has demonstrated,[6] were the foundation of his Platonic Academy. Almost all of the Platonists, both in Ficino's generation and later, were very explicit in their condemnation of the vice of homosexuality, with which men of letters had been taxed at least from the time of Dante's *Commedia*:

> In somma sappi che tutti fur cherci
> e litterati grandi e di gran fama,
> d'un peccato medesmo al mondo lerci.
> [*Inferno, canto* xv, *106-108*]

These are Brunetto Latini's words to Dante ("In short, know that all were great and renowned clerks and men of letters, stained on earth by one same sin").

Michelangelo's second biographer, Ascanio Condivi, writing in direct competition with Giorgio Vasari's famous, though inaccurate, biography, could vaunt his close association with the master. Indeed, it is quite probable that Michelangelo himself encouraged Condivi

23

in his task. Thus Condivi's account of Michelangelo's view of love and beauty may be accepted as authoritative:

"He [Michelangelo] has also loved bodily beauty, as one who knows it very well. Thus he has given occasion to certain carnal men, who are unable to understand the love of beauty in any but a lascivious and unchaste way, to think and speak evil of him— as though Alcibiades, a very handsome youth, had not been loved most chastely by Socrates. . . . I have several times heard Michelangelo talk about love; and then heard it said by those who were present that he spoke about it not otherwise than as Plato wrote. I never heard from his mouth any but the most chaste words. . . . [Furthermore,] he not only has loved human beauty, but universally every beautiful thing, a beautiful horse, a beautiful dog, a beautiful town, a beautiful plant, mountain, woods, admiring every beautiful thing and place with marvelous affection, thus taking beauty from nature as bees gather honey from flowers in order to use it in their work."[7]

A recent biographer, Giovanni Papini, one of Italy's best known literati in this century, goes to some length to refute the crude charge of pederasty levelled by Pietro Aretino, himself morally unblemished of course, and more recently repeated by such unbiased observers as Havelock Ellis and André Gide. Papini quotes these lines from Michelangelo:

> S' i' amo sol di te, signor mie caro,
> quel che di te più ami, non ti sdegni,
> chè l'un dell'altro spirto s'innamora.
> Quel che nel tuo bel volto bramo e 'mparo,
> e mal compres' è dagli umani ingegni,
> chi 'l vuol saper convien che prima mora.

If I love only that in you, my dear Lord, which you yourself most love, do not feel disdainful, for one spirit becomes enamored of the other. He who would know that which I crave and learn in your handsome face and which is poorly understood by human intellects, needs must first die.

Papini concludes with an animated defense of the "absolute purity" of Michelangelo's and Cavalieri's reciprocal affection, which he sees as "completely spiritual and almost sacred."[8]

However, a careful reading of Michelangelo's *Rime* in the context of what passed for Platonism in his times cannot support Papini's view. Contemporary writers widely repeated Ficino's classification of three kinds of love: divine, human, and bestial.[9] Divine love advances from the visual appreciation of the object of love to the contemplation of divine essences. Human love, also accepted as a moral pursuit and frequently identified in the sixteenth century with Petrarch's love of Laura, is that which continues to delight in seeing and conversing with the person loved. Bestial love, on the other hand, plunges from sight into what Ficino calls the "concupiscence of touch." Platonizing interpreters of Petrarch were embarrassed by Petrarch's more sensual expressions, which seemed to break the bounds of moral, human love:

> Con lei foss'io da che si parte il sole,
> E non ci vedess'altri che le stelle,
> Solo una notte! e mai non fosse l'alba. . . .
> [*Rime sparse* XXII, 31-33]

Would that I were with her from the setting of the sun, and that none saw us but the stars, one sole night, and it were never dawn.

Neither Condivi's nor Papini's defense of the spirituality of Michelangelo's passion will stand up when we read the following lines written by Michelangelo to Cavalieri, which Papini conveniently ignores:

O felice quel dì, se questo è certo!
Fermisi in un momento il tempo e l'ore,
il giorno e 'l sol nella su' antica traccia,
    acciò ch' i' abbi, e non già per mie merto,
il desïato mie dolce signore
per sempre nell'indegne e pronte braccia.
                                    [*Rime, 72*]

If this [your compassion toward me] is certain, how happy that day! May time and the hours, the day and the sun stop suddenly in their ancient track, so that, even if not by my own merit, I may hold forever in my undeserving and ready arms, my sweet, desired lord.

These lines, echoing Petrarch's most openly sensual utterance, are clearly not susceptible of Platonic interpretation in the sixteenth-century sense — nor, for that matter, in ours.

My own conclusion on this much-debated point is that Michelangelo wrote poems replete with overtones of Platonic philosophy to a handsome young man for whom he felt a passionate ardor, the intensity and sensuality of which were considerably greater than that allowed by his age to one who would call himself a Platonic lover. Some of Michelangelo's letters to Cavalieri tend to confirm this fact.[10]

There was another way, besides the intellectualization of love, in which the Renaissance Platonists could avoid the idea of homosexuality. Was it not possible that the passion of love, the dynamic for the ascent of Diotima's ladder, could be sparked not by a young man, but even by a young woman, someone not unlike Petrarch's golden-haired Laura? It could indeed! The first post-Ficinian Platonist clearly to choose this path was Pietro Bembo, eventually a Cardinal in the Roman Catholic Church — the same Bembo who canonized Petrarch and Boccaccio as the models for vernacular poetry and prose. Pietro Bembo, the immensely prestigious classicist from Venice who defended the literary excellence of the Tuscan vernacular, was soon to count many followers in the transformation of the philosophic love dialogue of Ficino and Leone Ebreo into a primarily literary topic of wide public appeal. During the sixteenth century the interpretation of Platonic myth and theory and the illustration of Platonic love by quotations from Petrarch were to become suitable subjects for Sunday afternoon lectures in Italian academies. The marriage of Neoplatonism with Neopetrarchism was celebrated — one cannot say "consummated" in this case — in Bembo's *Asolani*, published in 1505.

Thereafter the writing of sonnets and canzoni after the manner of Petrarch assumed epidemic proportions. I use the word advisedly; it was a disease. No one was to achieve in lyric poetry the Olympian heights of the master of Vaucluse. In the long century that runs from the appearance of Bembo to the tragic death of Giordano Bruno in 1600, only a few names stand out in the realm of the lyric: Torquato Tasso, Luigi Tansillo, Gaspara Stampa, perhaps Giovanni della Casa, Annibal Caro, Vittoria Colonna, and several others, but certainly also Michelangelo Buonarroti. None of them even remotely approach the level of excellence achieved in narrative poetry by Ariosto and Tasso. Those who stand out from the crowd do so by virtue of a rare, but unmistakable afflatus. Poetry is after all, as Plato said it was, a divine madness; and that divine madness was in Michelangelo Buonarroti.

Michelangelo's poems are not easy to read. Their texture is as rough as that of his unfinished *Prisoners* in the Accademia delle Belle Arti in Florence. I have not seen the autographs of his sonnets, but Girardi, who studied them carefully for his recent critical edition, tells us they sometimes show evidence of the haste with which he wrote down his first draft — frequently on a corner of some sketch, now on the back of a letter, now in the margin of a financial account. But to finish them — ah! that was another matter. Sometimes they were left unfinished. Sometimes a given line was rewritten as many as five or ten times. Even in their final state, one misses the even flow, the perfect diction of Petrarch and his most accomplished followers. The verbal energy comes out in irregular jets, so to speak, giving us for an instant the stark beauty and the incisiveness of a line from Dante, but resulting ultimately in flawed splendor. If we range through the volume of Michelangelo's poetry, picking a line here and a tercet there, we can easily delude ourselves into thinking that we have found a master poet. Perhaps this fact accounts for the awe and enthusiasm which his verse has inspired among foreign readers, notably in Germany. To find poems which are excellent in their entirety is more difficult. Compared with his sculptures and paintings, his poems have only a marginal importance. The very fact that he wrote them at all may be seen as an expression of the humanists' ideal of the universal man, which called forth verses of sorts even from the totally untrained Benvenuto Cellini. Michelangelo himself clearly separated his verse writing, wherein he was an amateur, from his professional activity as an artist. His biographer Condivi, a younger contemporary, wrote,

Since he takes great delight in the discussions of learned men, he has also derived pleasure from reading writers of both prose and verse, among whom he especially admires Dante, delighted by the wonderful intelligence of that man, whom he knows almost in his entirety. Yet he knows perhaps as much of Petrarch. And not only does he take pleasure in reading them, but in writing as well sometimes, as may be seen from some of his sonnets, which give excellent evidence of his great inventiveness and discernment. . . . But he does this more for his own pleasure than because he would make a profession of it, always disparaging himself and accusing his ignorance in these matters.[11]

The contortions and imperfections of Michelangelo's verses have been interpreted somewhat romantically as the same internal struggle between form and matter, spirit and flesh, which found expression in his sculpture and painting. A more realistic view of these imperfections would consider them simply the inevitable result of an inadequate literary education.

When Michelangelo began writing sonnets and letters to Vittoria Colonna, some time after their initial meeting, he was in his sixties and the famous poetess in her late forties. She replied to his letters, but despite the fact that she addressed verses to other poets of her time, she did not answer Michelangelo's sonnets. The overall picture of their relationship which one derives from their correspondence and from the poems that Michelangelo addressed to her is that of two ageing people "tied," as Vittoria says, "by a Christian knot of surest affection,"[12] engaged in a religious dialogue. For Michelangelo, Vittoria plays the role·of a mediatress between himself and the Divinity, not unlike that of the *donna angelicata*, or "angel-lady," of *stilnuovo* poetry. The following madrigal may be taken as typical:

S'egli è che 'l buon desio
porti dal mondo a Dio
alcuna cosa bella,
sol la mie donna è quella,
a chi ha gli occhi fatti com'ho io.
Ogni altra cosa oblio
e sol di tant'ho cura.
Non è gran maraviglia,
s'io l'amo e bramo e chiamo a tutte l'ore;
nè proprio valor mio,
se l'alma per natura
s'appoggia a chi somiglia
ne gli occhi gli occhi, ond'ella scende fore.
Se sente il primo amore
come suo fin, per quel qua questa onora:
c'amar diè 'l servo chi 'l signore adora.

[*Rime*, 117]

If it is true that good desire brings a thing of beauty from the world to God, only my lady can be *that*, to one who has eyes made like mine. I forget every other thing and care only for this. It is no great wonder if I love and desire and invoke her at every hour; nor is it my merit if my soul by nature finds support in her who in her eyes reflects the eyes through which my soul issues forth. If my soul feels primal Love as its end, it therefore honors here [on earth] this lady: for he who adores the lord must love the servant.

Michelangelo wrote many love poems that are addressed neither to Cavalieri nor to Vittoria Colonna. Some of them are excellent, and they show a fairly wide variation of tone. It would be interesting to know for whom they were intended, and whether some of them were merely literary exercises. We shall probably never know.

How moving, in another sonnet, is his tribute to Dante:

Di Dante dico, che mal conosciute
fur l'opre suo da quel popolo ingrato
che solo a iusti manca di salute.
    Fuss'io pur lui! c'a tal fortuna nato,
per l'aspro esilio suo, co' la virtute,
dare' del mondo il più felice stato.

[Rime, 248]

I speak of Dante, whose greatness was insufficiently recognized by that ungrateful people [the Florentine people] who denies its favor only to just men. O, would that I were he! Born as he was to such fortune, I would give up the happiest condition in the world in order to have his *virtù* [ability], and with it, face his harsh exile.

Here one great artist, fully conscious of his creative power, pays heartfelt homage to another, who was equally conscious of his own greatness. It would be rewarding to trace Michelangelo's debt to Dante — not only in his great paintings such as the Last Judgment, as German scholars did in the nineteenth century, but in his verses as well. But here we must be content with the mere observation that there are few if any poets in cinquecento Italy in whom Dante's presence is felt more strongly than in Michelangelo.

There remains yet another thread to mention in the tapestry of Michelangelo's *Rime*: those violent and bizarre poems of humor and ill humor in which, even when we least expect it, serious echoes resound. Consider these lines:

I' sto rinchiuso come la midolla,
de la sua scorza, qua pover e solo,
come spirto legato in un'ampolla:
    e la mia scura tomba è picciol volo,
dov'è Aragn' e mill'opre e lavoranti,

e fan di lor filando fusaiuolo.
   D'intorn'a l'uscio ho mete di giganti,
ché chi mangi' uva o ha presa medicina
non vanno altrove a cacar tutti quanti.
                                    [*Rime*, 267]

I am enclosed here like the wood inside its bark, poor and alone;
like spirits imprisoned in a vial; and my dark tomb is so small
that there is little room for flight. In it are Arachne and a thousand works and workers [in other words, a thousand spiders with
their webs] and they turn with their threads like so many spin-
ners. Around my door there is the excrement of giants, for all
those who eat grapes or take some medicine go nowhere else to
defecate.

That is just the beginning. And so he continues for another forty-six lines with ''gatti, carogne, . . . la tosse, il
freddo, . . . dilombato, crepato, infranto e rotto, . . . la
maniconia, . . . un calabron in un orciuolo, . . . in un orec-
chio un ragnatelo, . . .'' (''cats, carrion, . . . a cough, the
cold, . . . broken-backed, cracked, shattered, and broken,
. . . melancholy, . . . a hornet in a jug, . . . in an ear a
cobweb, . . .''). He concludes:

   L'arte pregiata, ov'alcun tempo fui
   di tant' opinion, mi rec' a questo,
   povero, vecchio e servo in forz'altrui,
      ch i' son disfatto, s' i' non muoro presto.

The prized art for which I once had so much fame has brought
me to this, poor, old and a slave to the will of others, so that I
am finished, if I don't die soon.

This *capitolo*, if formally it is humorous, contains a very
grim humor. Stark misery in old age, the feeling of neglected greatness — who has expressed them better? And
what pathos in the last line, ''ch' i' son disfatto, s' i' non

muoro presto'' (''for I am finished, if I don't die soon'')!

This is indeed a somber note on which to end our brief discussion of Michelangelo's poetry. We might have ended on the high note of the heaven-wafted flame of love. Yet it is not inappropriate to conclude with a note of contrast which will once again remind us of the overpowering humanity of Italy's greatest artist and of the variegated, ever-changing richness which characterizes the Italian Renaissance.

BY JOHN CHARLES NELSON

NOTES

1. Michelangiolo Buonarroti, *Rime,* ed. Enzo N. Girardi (Bari, 1960), p. 76. Subsequent references to this edition will appear in the text. The translations are mine.

2. *Vita di Michelangiolo nella vita del suo tempo* (Milan, 1955), p. 360.

3. *The Sonnets of Michael Angelo Buonarroti and Tommaso Campanella,* trans. John Addington Symonds (London, 1878), p. 73.

4. Papini, p. 355.

5. "Il Raverta," in *Trattati d'amore del cinquecento,* ed. G. Zonta (Bari, 1912), p. 10.

6. Paul Oskar Kristeller, *The Philosophy of Marsilio Ficino* (New York, 1943), p. 208.

7. *Vita di Michelangiolo Buonarroti, pittore, scultore, architetto e gentiluomo fiorentino* (Florence, 1746), pp. 98-99.

8. Papini, p. 304.

9. Marsilio Ficino, *Sopra lo amore o ver' Convito di Platone* (Florence, 1544).

10. See, for example, his letter of July 28, 1553, with its variants, in *Le Lettere di Michelangelo Buonarroti,* ed. Gaetano Milanesi (Florence, 1875), pp. 467-68, and *The Letters of Michelangelo,* trans. E. H. Ramsden (London, 1963), 1, 184. There is insufficient documentary evidence for reaching conclusions about Michelangelo's private conduct. Conjectures of a psychosexual nature which have been drawn from Michelangelo's art are fairly well known and lie beyond the subject of this paper, which is Michelangelo's poetry.

11. Condivi, p. 98.

12. *Carteggio,* ed. Ermanno Ferrero and Giuseppe Müller, 2nd ed. (Florence and Rome, 1892), Letter CLVII.

BIBLIOGRAPHY

Bembo, Pietro. *Gli Asolani e le Rime,* ed. Carlo Dionisotti-Casalone. Turin, 1932.

Betussi, Giuseppe. "Il Raverta," in *Trattati d'amore del cinquecento,* ed. G. Zonta. Bari, 1912, pp. 1-150.

Buonarroti, Michelangelo. *The Complete Poems of Michelangelo,* trans. Joseph Tusiani. New York, 1960.

————. *The Letters of Michelangelo,* trans. and ed. E. H. Ramsden. 2 vols. London, 1963.

————. *Le rime di Michelangelo Buonarroti, pittore, scultore e architetto . . . ,* ed. Cesare Guasti. Florence, 1863.

————. *Rime,* ed. Enzo N. Girardi. Bari, 1960.

————. *The Sonnets,* trans. John Addington Symonds. New York, 1948.

Clements, Robert John. *The Poetry of Michelangelo.* New York, 1965.

Condivi, Ascanio. *Vita di Michelangiolo Buonarroti, pittore, scultore, architetto e gentiluomo fiorentino.* Florence, 1746.

Dante Alighieri. *La divina commedia.* Florence, 1921.

Farinelli, Arturo. *Michelangelo e Dante e altri brevi saggi.* Turin, 1918.

Flamini, Francesco. *Il cinquecento.* Milan, 1898-1902.

Kristeller, Paul Oskar. *The Philosophy of Marsilio Ficino.* New York, 1943.

Nelson, John Charles. *Renaissance Theory of Love.* New York, 1958.

Papini, Giovanni. *Michelangelo, his Life and his Era,* trans. Loretta Murnane. New York, 1952.

Petrarca, Francesco. *Le Rime.* Bologna, 1964.

Robb, Nesca A. *Neoplatonism of the Italian Renaissance.* London, 1935.

Valency, Maurice. *In Praise of Love.* New York, 1961.

Varchi, Benedetto. *Due Lezzioni . . . , nella prima delle quali si dichiara un sonetto di messer Michelangelo Buonarroti.* Florence, 1549.

Vasari, Giorgio. *La Vita di Michelangelo nelle redazioni del 1550 e del 1568,* ed. Paola Barocchi. 5 vols. Milan, 1962.

The Flavor of Early Renaissance Technology

ecently the emergence of two long-neglected manuscripts of Leonardo da Vinci in Madrid,[1] one of them an immensely exciting unfinished treatise on machine design which Leonardo was clearly preparing for publication, has focused new attention on the nature and style of technology in the early Renaissance. Even scholars whose primary concerns are with the literature, politics, art, philosophy, or religion of the fourteenth and fifteenth centuries are beginning to realize that in engineering likewise the men of that age displayed the sort of creativity which we have come to expect of them.

The field is filled with surprises. Some years ago in Florence I looked at Biblioteca Nazionale, MS B. R. 228, the unpublished, technological notebook dating from the 1480s of Buonaccorso Ghiberti, the grandson of Lorenzo Ghiberti. I was so fascinated to find in it (on folio 113v) what I believe to be the first groove cam — an essential device in the history of automation — that I stupidly overlooked the choicest morsel. Unknown to me, Gustina

Scaglia of Queen's College, New York, had seen that certain of these sketches preserve the design of the great derrick which Brunelleschi built around 1421 to aid the construction of the dome of the Florentine cathedral.[2] Unknown either to Scaglia or to me, Ladislao Reti, then of São Paulo, had made the same identification. But Reti, being technically trained as an engineer, could see things that Scaglia, an art historian, could see less easily. At the margin of a detail of this derrick he found a notation indicating that under the wheels illustrated there were other wheels. From his professional knowledge of machinery Reti immediately understood how the apparatus worked, and the toolmakers of his chemical factory in Brazil built a model of it. The result is a far more sophisticated hoist than anyone had thought possible in the early fifteenth century.

* * *

A great obstacle to the appraisal of this phase of Renaissance culture is the dearth of scholarly work in the field. Theodor Beck's *Beiträge zur Geschichte des Maschinenbaues*, published in 1899 at Berlin, remains the most satisfactory description of the work of certain individual engineers of the early Renaissance, but Beck failed to locate many of the extant manuscripts. William B. Parsons's *Engineers and Engineering in the Renaissance*, which appeared at Baltimore in 1939, is useful. Bertrand Gille's *Engénieurs de la Renaissance*[3] is chiefly valuable for its inventory of manuscripts, but even this needs revision.[4]

Save for Alberti, Francesco di Giorgio, Filarete, and Leonardo, little work has been done on the biographies of Renaissance technologists, and when (as was normal until the early sixteenth century) engineers were also artists, their lives have been written in the context of their painting, sculpture, or architecture rather than with an eye to their engineering. As Reti remarked to me after he first looked at the Madrid manuscripts, "Now at last people will begin to believe me when I tell them that Leonardo was an engineer who occasionally painted a picture when he was broke."

There are many unexplored sources for the lives of such men. I had been interested for thirty years in Jacopo Aconcio as a theologian before, thanks to C. D. O'Malley's biography of him,[5] I learned that he made his living as an engineer. O'Malley, however, had been unable to discover many details about his professional career. Thanks to an overlooked memorandum in the British Museum, I was able to do something to fill that lacuna.[6] I have every confidence that further materials, including a copy of his vanished *Ars muniendorum oppidorum*, will be found as soon as a considerable group of scholars becomes aware that such problems exist.

The chief need is for careful publication of the notebooks of the engineers of the period. Villard de Honnecourt's very important sketchbook of ca. 1235 has long been available in H. R. Hahnloser's edition issued at Vienna in 1935[7]. But, because few scholars combine the necessary palaeographic and linguistic skills with technical insight, many writings remain unedited from the later period.

For example, while Rupert Hall of London has long promised to produce an edition of Guido da Vigevano's *Texaurus* of 1335,[8] he has not yet managed it. The vocabulary is not easy: as Hall said to me, "It's as though blacksmiths and shipwrights were talking Latin." But, of course, blacksmiths and shipwrights once did talk Latin, and this adds to the philological interest of the text. Guido was a Lombard who was personal physician first to the German Emperor and then to the Queen of France. His *Texaurus*, written in Paris, exhorts the king to launch a new Crusade to redeem the Holy Places from Islam. As a physician Guido knew that the earlier expeditions had been defeated as much by disease as by the prowess of the Infidels; so the first section of the book is medical. The second part, however, describes and illustrates a variety of siege machines and the like which apparently he himself had invented and which he believed would be effective in the campaign. Some of his designs, such as a siege tower self-propelled by windmills, are fantastic; but the book contains important original elements, notably the first compound cranks and a great emphasis on apparatus consisting of demountable, interchangeable parts which can be easily transported. Whether Guido drew on prior Italian sources unknown to us, or whether his work influenced later engineers directly, is uncertain. However, some drawings by the Sienese engineers of the fifteenth century, and those appearing in Roberto Valturio's *De re militare* of the 1450s, are clearly in some way related to Guido's pictures.

In Central Europe the engineering tradition was dominated from 1405 onward for a century and a half by Konrad Kyeser's *Bellifortis* which is now available in facsimile with an annotated transcription.[9] To my own eye, the still unedited notebook of the 1430s produced by an anonymous German engineer of the Hussite Wars[10] is even more provocative, while the anonymous *Mittelalterliche Hausbuch* of the 1480s produced by a superb artist who had a passionate interest in the advancing technology of his time — he shows (folio 34a) the flyer on a spinning wheel even earlier than Leonardo — is one of the great documents of the Northern Renaissance, but neglected despite an admirable facsimile edition. Those still afflicted with the Platonic and Romantic conviction — unknown in the Middle Ages or Renaissance — that engines and human values are necessarily at odds, should ponder an elaborate double-page drawing in this manuscript: youths and maidens crowned with wreaths are sporting in a pleasure garden dominated by a fountain, while, at the right, quite unobscured, one sees the water-driven force pump which makes the fountain play.[11] In that age, machinery was integral to the arts, as all the arts were essential to the good life.

In the fifteenth century, however, the technology of Italy was even richer than that of Germany, yet its records are little known. The lavishly illustrated notebook of Giovanni Fontana preserved in Munich (Staatsbibliothek, Codex icon. 242) has been scantily examined. From the 1440s until the 1480s, Siena, which was best rep-resented by Mariano di Jacopo detto il Taccola and by Francesco di Giorgio, seems to have been the chief source of innovation.

The manuscripts of the Sienese school are numerous and confusing. In addition to works of Taccola and of Francesco, others may be either later recensions by these masters, or else notebooks of their disciples. Typical of this rich chaos is a British Museum sketchbook of the 1470s or early 1480s (see *infra*, n. 44) which no one seems to have noticed. Its first thirty-one folios are in effect identical with Florence, Biblioteca Nazionale, Palat. 766

which Taccola signed and dated 13 January 1433. The rest of the 198 lavishly illustrated folios are generally in the Francesco di Giorgio tradition (he is mentioned on folios 129^r and 194^v) but contain curious items which seem to be original. Until we unscramble the relations between the many intricate and exuberant manuscripts which show primarily the Sienese style in engineering,[12] we shall not have solved the central documentary problems of Renaissance technology.

In 1477 when Francesco di Giorgio left Siena to become the chief engineer of Federigo da Montefeltro, the court of Urbino became briefly a center of intense technological interest, a fact best symbolized by the seventy-two magnificent marble reliefs of pumps, sawmills, war machines, and the like, designed by Francesco, which decorate the ducal palace of that city.[13] It is no accident that Polydore Vergil, who was educated in Urbino during that burst of vitality, produced in his *De inventoribus rerum* of 1499 the first extensive modern effort to explore the history of technology.[14]

In the later 1480s the new technology became more diffused. For nearly a century thereafter Italian engineers scattered over Europe, from Madrid to Moscow and back to Britain, monopolizing the best jobs, erecting wonderful new machines, building palaces and fortifications, and helping to bankrupt every government which hired them. To tax-paying natives they were a plague of locusts, but rulers in the sixteenth century considered them indispensable. Their impact upon the general culture of Europe was as great as that of the contemporary Italian humanists, artists, and musicians, yet their history remains completely unwritten.[15] This is the greatest single lacuna in our understanding of the diffusion of the Italian Renaissance.

                              *   *   *

In the twentieth century we assume that an advancing technology must consist essentially of practical application of scientific discovery. Moreover, it is now clear that from the middle of the thirteenth century onward there was a notable scientific movement in Western Europe which, indeed, built on the Greek and Arabic inheritance but which quickly achieved original and significant results. A priori it would follow that the vigor of late medieval and early Renaissance technology was closely related to the scientific advance of the period.

We should beware, however, of interpreting former centuries according to more recent patterns of relationships. Let us look at some specific problems.

In 1269 Peter of Maricourt, a military engineer whom Friar Roger Bacon considered the greatest scientist of his time, was employed in the retinue of Charles of Anjou at the siege of Lucera, a Muslim garrison established by the Hohenstaufens in South Italy. The site was strong, and the place could only be starved into submission. To pass the time, Peter composed his *Epistola de magnete*,[16] which in 1600 William Gilbert made the basis of his *De magnete* and which is therefore the cornerstone of all modern work in magnetism and electricity. The *Epistola* is based on Peter's observation of compass makers at work, the nautical compass having been introduced to Europe from China some seventy-five years earlier.[17] The occasion and context for this very theoretical analysis of magnetism is thus a technological innovation rather than the reverse. Nevertheless, at the end of the *Epistola* Peter of Maricourt attempts two novel engineering applications of the magnetic force which he is trying to understand. One is a perpetual motion wheel turned by magnetism. The second is a sphere of magnetic iron mounted without friction parallel to the axis of the heavens. He believes that it will rotate in sympathy with the celestial spheres once every twenty-four hours, thus, as he says, making all other forms of clocks obsolete. That neither of these devices would work is irrelevant: the significant fact is that Peter of Maricourt, starting from a new technological device, laid the foundations of a novel science and then attempted engineering applications of what he had found. This sounds very modern; but we should be cautious.

Peter belonged to the first generation of scientists who, perhaps beginning with Robert Grosseteste, used lenses in the study of optics, with admirable scientific results. Indeed, it will be recalled that about 1266 Roger Bacon sent to the Pope a lens that had been made by a friend of his in Paris.[18] In the early 1280s eyeglasses were invented in the region of Pisa or Lucca,[19] and their use spread swiftly, in Italy at least, to the point where in 1306 a preacher in Florence could refer to the making of spectacles as "one of the most useful and necessary arts in the world."[20] There is no proof that the invention of eyeglasses was directly the result of the contemporary scientific interest in lenses. It seems more probable that both were separate outgrowths of a remarkable development of the glass industries in the late thirteenth century, particularly the Italian discovery of clear optical glass and new methods of cutting glass, gems, and crystal.[21] The mood in which, in the *Roman de la Rose*, Jean de Meung, a learned man, about 1277 extols the marvels both of lenses and of the new mirrors of silvered glass[22] indicates that such practical achievements were not rooted in the new science, although the new science might explain them as phenomena.

By the later thirteenth century, however, one group of scientifically educated men was becoming intensely concerned with a specific problem of machine design: how to build a mechanical clock. The translation of Hellenistic and Muslim works had led to a great growth of interest in astrology. The casting of horoscopes became essential to the diagnosis and treatment of disease, with the result that every first-rate physician was also an astronomer. Exact observation of the transit of heavenly bodies, however, was exasperatingly difficult with waterclocks: even when, on chilly nights, they did not freeze entirely, their outlets tended to coat with ice, altering the volume of flow. Obviously a better timing device must be found.

There were several proposals. We have already noted Peter of Maricourt's notion in 1269 of a rotating magnetic sphere: he specifically suggests that a star map be engraved upon it to help celestial observations. In the 1270s, writing under the patronage of Alfonso el Sabio of Castile, Rabbi Isaac ben Sid described as an absolute novelty a clock consisting of a drum rotated by a falling weight, the escapement being provided by mercury flowing through small holes from compartment to compartment within the drum.[23] This is entirely feasible and established a whole species of timepieces.[24] But it seems not to have become popular.

Someone began experimenting with what we wrongly call the sand glass. Sand is not suitable in such devices because it quickly abrades the small hole through which it flows. Not until the early fourteenth century was this problem solved by developing, so it would seem, the normal flowing substance of such instruments: finely pulverized eggshell.[25] But while these timekeepers were useful on ships because rough seas did not affect them, they did not help astronomers or physicians because the powder falling into the lower container does not assume a level for exact measurement of time in observation of the stars.

As early as about 1271 a fourth possible solution was suggested by Robert the Englishman: he describes with enthusiasm how to wrap a rope around an axle of a dial in such a way that a weight at the end of the rope will rotate the axle and the dial exactly once a day.[26] He admits, however, that not all the difficulties have been mastered in this machine; in other words, the mechanical escapement is a dream but not yet an actuality. Obviously, all over Europe men with adventurous minds were trying to solve this problem. It took them sixty years or more: there is no firm evidence of the mechanical escapement in either the wheel or the verge form until 1341, when it was so well known in Milan that weight-driven mills for grinding grain were being invented on its analogy.[27]

Considering the medical incentives to the invention of the mechanical clock, it is not astonishing that the most extraordinary planetary and calendrical clock of the fourteenth century was completed in 1364, after sixteen years of labor, by a professor of medicine and astronomy at the Universities of Pavia and Padua, Giovanni de' Dondi, called by contemporaries, for his accomplishment, Giovanni dall' Orologio.[28] That he left us a massive descriptive text and such elaborate diagrams of it that a full-scale working model now may be seen in

Washington is perhaps less unexpected than the fact that he made the clock with his own hands. We remember that Guido da Vigevano, another famous physician of the same generation, wrote a book of his own inventions. Konrad Kyeser had a medical education and his *Bellifortis* is introduced by an astrological procession of the planets. It would appear that the combination of medicine with astronomy in the early Renaissance, and astronomy's need for a mechanical clock, led at least some physicians to sophisticated manual experiments in machine construction. Thus there was in this instance a relation between technology and science, but it was far from the normal modern relation. Technology advanced by supplying the instrumental needs of science; it did not advance by application of scientific discovery.

It is sometimes said that the engineers and architects of the Middle Ages and Renaissance, like those of antiquity, applied the mathematics of proportion to their products, and that this is technology stemming from science. If one wishes to make either a building or a pile driver half again as big as an existing building or pile driver, one makes all the measurements half again as big. Surely, however, this is straight empiricism rather than applied science.

A somewhat better case can be made for the new Italian style of fortification which began to emerge from the drawing boards into actuality about 1530.[29] By the 1490s easily mobile cannons shooting iron balls in a flat arc had been developed which shattered the most massive walls. Since breeching could no longer be prevented, the problem became how to block the storming of the inevitable breech. The answer was found in the new triangular bastion, shaped like the head of an arrow, with casemates, protected by the tangs of the arrow, from which guns could sweep the curtain wall and slaughter the attackers.

It was a profound shock to the thinking of Europe to discover that military security in a fortress now depended less on lofty masonry or strength of position than upon careful calculation of lines of fire. Indeed, the daring Italian engineers who propagated the new method preferred flat sites where no accident of terrain interfered with their geometrizing. Every sixteenth-century treatise on the art of fortification insists that mathematics is its essence, and unquestionably the new respect for mathematics fostered by the brutal exigencies of war helped to prepare the European mind for the Galilean-Cartesian notion that mathematics is the primary way of discovering and describing reality. Nevertheless, when one looks at the novel military works of that age, one concludes that pure calculation was seldom possible: the military engineers of the sixteenth century had new skills, but despite all the talk about theory, their methods were essentially empirical.

Only one other claim has been seriously made for an early Renaissance application of science to practical affairs. As the Portuguese mariners of the fifteenth century worked their way down the coast of Africa and into the South Atlantic searching for a sea route to India, the polestar ceased to be an aid to navigation. Some have asserted that Italian astronomers worked out a new method of astronomical navigation to guide ships in low latitudes and in the southern hemisphere. It is now recognized, however, (1) that this sort of astronomical navigation was not used by Mediterranean sailors until a century after the seamen of the Atlantic were applying it; and (2) that the Muslim pilot who steered Vasco da Gama's ship from the African coast to Calicut in 1497 was using methods very like those of the Portuguese.[30] It is hard to believe that Arabic or Indic science on the one hand, and Portuguese science on the other, had been independently applied to navigational problems, while both the scientists and the sailors of the Mediterranean remained ignorant of the double process. It is somewhat easier to believe that the skilled navigators of both the Indian Ocean and the South Atlantic, faced with an identical problem, solved it empirically in similar ways.

The bursting of Europe's oceanic boundaries at the end of the fifteenth century is one of the central events in history. It was made possible by a long and ingenious series of medieval and Renaissance improvements in ship-building and the nautical arts which were entirely em-pirical. The majestic result is the measure of the possible effectiveness of such empiricism. Historians should not exaggerate the power of theory.

* * *

There is a second assumption prevalent in our time which should be examined: the idea that the prime source of vigor in the Renaissance was the discovery of classical antiquity. How much classical stimulus can be found in Renaissance technology?

The answer would seem to be: none. Taccola, the famous engineer of Siena, was nicknamed "Archimedes," presumably because Europe remembered the story of the military machines which the ancient Syracusan built to defend his city. The substance of Archimedes' works was known to scientists in the later Middle Ages,[31] but nothing of his that survives is technological. Vitruvius, who had never been forgotten,[32] enjoyed a great new vogue in the fifteenth century not because of his engineering, but because his description of the classic architectural orders helped to implement the humanist revolt against gothic taste. Hero of Alexandria's treatises on machines remained untranslated until the later sixteenth century, presumably because, as the automata of European clocks showed, the West had worked out more satisfactory mechanical ways of achieving the same ends.

Indeed, it is hard to see what antiquity had to teach the technicians of the fourteenth and fifteenth centuries. While the remarkable gearing of the Antikithera fragment,[33] dating from the first century B.C., shows that the Hellenistic age was capable of a sophistication in machine design of which the written records provide no evidence, it does not surpass medieval clocks in skill. The glory of Greece and Rome was only in small measure technological. Indeed, one reason why Roman ruins are so visually impressive is that the Romans were clumsy engineers: they had little sense of economy of means; their masonry was vastly more massive than was necessary. Only one device known to the ancient world seems to have been forgotten subsequently until it was consciously revived through humanist influence: the hodometer. Vitruvius describes one, and a modernized form of it is pictured in the Como 1521 edition of that author.

In the late fourteenth and fifteenth centuries, in Italy at least, the concept of a fertilizing classical Renaissance may usefully be applied to understanding the visual arts, belles lettres, certain areas of philosophy, historiography, and a few other kinds of activity. But to technology, as to economics and the development of social structures, it is irrelevant. Terms like antiquity, the Middle Ages, or modern times are conceptually fairly neutral; the word *Renaissance,* in contrast, states a thesis about the nature of the period which is unfortunate because it names the whole for a part. Nevertheless *Renaissance* is now so deeply embedded in bibliography, college catalogues, and institutional names that it may long outlive the interpretation of history which produced it. Moreover, we still have no better name for that wonderfully creative period which was no longer quite medieval but was not yet quite modern.

* * *

If the innovative quality of Renaissance engineering is to be credited neither to application of scientific discovery nor to stimulus from antiquity, the final hypothesis might be that it reflected the new needs of a rapidly expanding commercial society and of monarchs eager to increase not only their armed might but also the prosperity of their realms.

Burghers and tyrants did, indeed, value engineers: Leonardo, for example, worked as such for the Duke of Milan, for Cesare Borgia, for the Florentine republic, and for Francis I. Obviously, technicians would not have been maintained, often in affluence, if they had not normally met the demands of their patrons. Yet, as one looks at their manuscript notebooks, and at the published engineering works which began to appear in the second half of the sixteenth century, the impression is not utilitarian. Quite the contrary, the engineers seem most often to be indulging in a speculative empiricism which is almost playful in flavor.

From the time of the Sienese school until at least Agostino Ramelli's great book of machines, published at Paris in 1588, engineers delighted in recording, for example, every possible variation in water mills which they could imagine. One will find sequences of pages filled with dozens of different designs of devices for scaling walls, or of portable military bridges, or of pumps or weight-lifting machines. Men of that age had to pump water and scale walls; but such elaboration of alternate methods clearly goes beyond utility: for the pure fun of discovery these engineers were exploring how many ways one could skin a cat.

In fact, some of their most fascinating insights have no relation to contemporary needs. Clack valves, metal discs hinged at one side, had been known since antiquity. In the Gabinetto dei Disegni at the Uffizi, among the papers of Antonio da San Gallo the Younger, I found four sketches, datable in the 1530s on the basis of watermarks, which show what I believe to be the earliest spherical valves.[34] So far as the Occident is concerned, the conical valve first appears in Leonardo's notebooks, but Ladislao Reti has noted that it does not enter the general literature of technology until 1588 with Ramelli's book.[35] That Ramelli looked on conical valves as very new and desirable is shown by both a drawing and a rejected plate at the University of California, Los Angeles,[36] preparatory for Ramelli's final illustration of a pump. Spherical valves are shown both in the initial sketch and in the discarded print; but then, at what must have been considerable expense, the whole picture was redrawn and reengraved for

Ramelli's plate 3 in order to substitute conical for spherical valves.

Those who know more about engineering than I do, tell me that the clack valve is entirely satisfactory until one is dealing with liquids or gases under high pressures or travelling at great speeds. No Renaissance engineer had to cope with such conditions. Not until steam began to be harnessed two centuries or more after Leonardo and San Gallo were new valves needed. But, thanks to the non-utilitarian, conceptual adventures of the Italians, a repertory of valves was available when the eighteenth century required them. Today, when our society depends so greatly on natural gas and oil travelling in pipelines over vast distances at high pressures, we may contemplate with gratitude the Renaissance expansion of the variety of valves.

Another illustration may help to prove my point. The later Middle Ages and early Renaissance were much interested in the uses of air. About 1010 an Anglo-Saxon Benedictine monk named Eilmer built a glider, took off from the tower of Malmesbury Abbey, and flew 600 feet. He crashed because, according to his own diagnosis, he forgot to put a tail on the rear end — "caudam in posteriore parte."[37] In the later twelfth century the horizontal-axle windmill appeared in the North Sea region and spread with amazing rapidity.[38] Perhaps by the middle of the thirteenth century and certainly in the fourteenth century,[39] the resistance of air was being used in fan escapements to slow the fall of the weight in striking trains, first of water clocks and then of mechanical clocks. By 1425 the blowgun had reached Europe from Indonesia bringing its Malay name with it (Malay, *sumpitan*; Arabic, *zabaṭāna*; Italian, *cerbottana*; English, *sarbacand*),

and this led to experiments with air guns and air pressures.[40] A 1474 Nuremberg picture shows a winehandler using a specialized bellows to force wine through a tube from one cask to another:[41] the earliest instance of the use of air pressure to transport materials. In Taccola's notebook of the 1430s[42] appears the first of several fifteenth-century pictures of a child's whirligig top, perhaps borrowed from China,[43] which at the end of the century inspired Leonardo's extraordinary helicopter design.

It has been universally said that Leonardo likewise was the first to think of decelerating the fall of a man by friction of the air with a parachute. However, slightly before Leonardo there were relevant drawings which may be found in the British Museum's hitherto unnoticed manuscript of the Sienese school mentioned above (p. 40).[44] On folio 189^v we see a man jumping. In his teeth he holds a sponge to protect his jaws from the shock of landing. His fall is being braked by long cloth streamers attached to his belt. He looks frightened, and he should be. The next few folios show the usual hoists, military machines, and the like. But the engineer drawing those pictures was getting worried about the jumper, whose situation was perilous. Something better had to be done for him. So, on folio 200^v, he appears again. The sponge is now held in his teeth by a strap around his head so that if he cries out in terror he will not drop it. And over his head, in place of the streamers, is a conical parachute: the first, I believe.

Leonardo's parachute was pyramidal rather than conical. We shall never know whether he saw the British Museum sketch, and it is not a question of great importance.

Renaissance engineers lived in a world of excited oral communication:[45] by the 1480s the idea of the parachute, if not the thing itself, was in the air. It reached publication in the early seventeenth century in the famous book of machines by Fausto Veranzio, a Dalmatian bishop.[46]

It may be doubted whether our anonymous engineer really believed that his parachute would work: it was too small to sustain a man's weight; but so were those of Leonardo and Veranzio. For some 300 years after the conceptual invention of the parachute, no one actually jumped in one. Then, when ballooning made parachuting functional, the idea was waiting to be used.

Today, when the parachute is fundamental both to military operations and to the retrieval of vehicles for the exploration of outer space, we may well be a bit awed by the empirical genius of the unknown Renaissance engineer who invented it. If we are to catch the distinctive flavor of his work, and of the others in his age, we must recognize that they were practical men earning their livings by doing concrete jobs for their employers. Nevertheless, by transcending what was practical in their own day, they helped decisively to build this distant future in which we live.

BY LYNN WHITE, JR.

NOTES

1. Ladislao Reti, "The Two Unpublished Manuscripts of Leonardo da Vinci in the Biblioteca Nacional of Madrid, I," *Burlington Magazine,* CX (1968), 10-22.

2. G. Scaglia, "Drawings of Brunelleschi's Mechanical Inventions for the Construction of the Cupola," *Marsyas,* X (1960-61), 45-67; see also Ladislao Reti, *Tracce dei progetti perduti di Filippo Brunelleschi nel Codice Atlantico di Leonardo da Vinci* [IV *Lettura Vinciana*] (Florence, 1965).

3. (Paris, 1964); Eng. tr. (Cambridge, Mass., 1965).

4. See my review in *Renaissance Quarterly,* XXI (1968), 39-42, and on the general topic: Friedrich Klemm, "Die Rolle der Technik in der italienischen Renaissance," *Technikgeschichte,* XXXIII (1965), 221-43.

5. *Jacopo Aconcio* (Rome, 1955).

6. Lynn White, jr., "Jacopo Aconcio as an Engineer," *American Historical Review,* LXXII (1967), 425-44.

7. See also the less copious *Sketchbook of Villard de Honnecourt,* ed. T. Bowie (Bloomington, Ind., 1959).

8. A. R. Hall, "The Military Inventions of Guido da Vigevano," in *Actes du VIIᵉ Congrès International d'Histoire des Sciences* (Florence, 1958), pp. 966-69.

9. Two vols., ed. Götz Quarg (Düsseldorf, 1967).

10. Munich, Staatsbibliothek, Codex latinus 197.

11. *Das mittelalterliche Hausbuch,* ed. H. T. Bossert and W. F. Storck (Leipzig, 1912), fol. 24ᵛ-25ʳ.

12. A firm basis for such studies has now been provided by Corrado Maltese's edition of Francesco di Giorgio's *Trattati di architettura, ingegneria e arte militare,* 2 vols. (Milan, 1967). An example of personal contact between engineers of this period is provided by Frank D. Prager, "A Manuscript of Taccola, Quoting Brunelleschi, on Problems of Inventors and Builders," *Proceedings of the American Philosophical Society,* CXII (1968), 131-49.

13. Gerhard Eimer, "Francesco di Giorgios Fassadenfries am Herzogspalast zu Urbino," *Festschrift Ulrich Middeldorf* (Berlin, 1968), pp. 187-98.

14. Alex Keller, "A Renaissance Humanist Looks at 'New' Inventions: The Article 'Horologium' in Giovanni Tortelli's De orthographia," *Technology and Culture,* XI (1970), 345-65, shows that Vergil's inventory was largely based on one produced about 1450 by a humanist at the papal court.

15. A quantity of biographical material, but subject to much correction and lacking synthesis, is contained in the writings of Carlo Promis chiefly published in *Miscellanea di storia italiana,* I (1862), 105-43; IV (1863), 359-442, 579-689; VI (1865), 241-356; XII (1871), 411-735; XIV (1874), 1-858; see also L. A. Maggiorotti, *Architetti e architettura militari,* 2 vols. (Rome, 1933-36).

16. *Epistola Petri Peregrini de Maricourt ad Sygerium de Foucaucourt militem,* in Gustav Hellmann, ed., *Rara magnetica* (Berlin, 1898).

17. Lynn White, jr., *Medieval Technology and Social Change* (Oxford, 1962), p. 132.

18. R. Bacon, *Opera quaedam hactenus inedita*, ed. J. S. Brewer (London, 1859), p. III.

19. E. Rosen, "The Invention of Eyeglasses," *Journal of the History of Medicine and Allied Sciences*, XI (1956), 13-46.

20. Robert Davidsohn, *Storia di Firenze*, VI (Florence, 1965), 22.

21. See A. Gasparetto, *Il vetro di Murano* (Venice, 1958), pp. 59-61; H. R. Hahnloser, "Schola et artes cristellariorum de Veneciis, 1284-1319," in *Venezia e l'Europa, Atti del XVIII Congresso Internazionale di Storia dell'Arte* (Venice, 1956), pp. 157-65.

22. *Le roman de la rose*, ed. E. Langlois, 5 vols. (Paris, 1914-24), lines 18044-18077, 18153-18294.

23. *Libros del saber de astronomia del re D. Alfonso de Castilla*, ed. M. Rico y Sinobas (Madrid, 1866), IV, 67-76.

24. Silvio A. Bedini, "The Compartmented Cylindrical Clepsydra," *Technology and Culture*, III (1962), 115-41.

25. C. B. Drover, "Sandglass 'Sand,' " *Antiquarian Horology*, III (1960), 62-67.

26. Lynn Thorndike, "Invention of the Mechanical Clock about 1271 A.D.," *Speculum*, XVI (1941), 242-43.

27. White, *Medieval Technology*, p. 124.

28. Giovanni Dondi dall' Orologio, *Tractatus astrarii*, ed. A. Barzon, E. Morpurgo, A. Petrucci, and G. Francescato (Vatican City, 1960).

29. The best study is that by J. R. Hale, "The Early Development of the Bastion: An Italian Chronology, c. 1450-c. 1534," in *Europe in the Late Middle Ages*, ed. J. R. Hale, et al. (Evanston, Ill., 1965), pp. 466-94.

30. A. Teixeira da Mota, "L'art de naviguer en Méditerranée du XIIIe au XVIIe siècle et la creation de la navigation astronomique dans les océans," in *Le navire et l'économie maritime du moyen-âge au XVIIIe siècle principalement en Méditerranée*, ed. M. Mollat (Paris, 1958), pp. 127-40.

31. See Marshall Clagett, *Archimedes in the Middle Ages, I: The Arabo-Latin Tradition* (Madison, Wisc., 1964).

32. Lucia A. Ciapponi, "Il *De architectura* di Vitruvio nel primo umanesimo," *Italia medioevale e umanistica*, III (1960), 59-99.

33. Derek J. de S. Price, "An Ancient Greek Computer," *Scientific American*, CC (June, 1959), 60-67.

34. Uffizi drawings Nos. 294, 847, 1468, 1493.

35. Ladislao Reti, "A Postscript to the Filarete Discussion: On Horizontal Waterwheels and Smelter Blowers in the Writings of Leonardo da Vinci and Juanello Turriano," *Technology and Culture*, VI (1965), 441.

36. The drawing is fol. 104^r, and the rejected plate is fol. 99^r, both bound in the second section of the second copy of Ramelli in the Special Collections

of the Library of the University of California, Los Angeles. Wilbur Smith, Director of Special Collections, first noted the drawing; John Arnold, a graduate student, found the variant plate.

37. Lynn White, jr., "Eilmer of Malmesbury, an Eleventh Century Aviator: A Case Study of Technological Innovation, Its Context and Tradition," *Technology and Culture*, II (1961), 97-111.

38. White, *Medieval Technology*, pp. 87-88.

39. Ibid., p. 121, Fig. 10.

40. Lynn White, jr., "Tibet, India and Malaya as Sources of Western Medieval Technology," *American Historical Review*, LXV (1960), 521-22.

41. *Das Hausbuch der Mendelschen Zwölfbrüderstiftung zu Nürnberg* ed. W. Treue et al. (Munich, 1965), Bilderband, Plate 143.

42. Ladislao Reti, "Helicopters and Whirligigs," *Raccolta Vinciana*, XX (1964), 331-38.

43. Joseph Needham, *Science and Civilization in China*, Vol. IV, Part 2 of *Mechanical Engineering* (Cambridge, Eng., 1965), pp. 580-85.

44. Lynn White, jr., "The Invention of the Parachute," *Technology and Culture* IX (July, 1968), 462-67.

45. White, "Aconcio," 440-41.

46. Fausto Veranzio, *Machinae novae* (Venice, [1615-1616]), pl. 38. For the date of publication, see Friedrich Klemm's appendix to the facsimile edition (Munich, 1965).

BIBLIOGRAPHY

There is no unified discussion of the technology of the Renaissance. The closest approach is Umberto Forti, *Storia della tecnica dal Medioevo al Rinascimento* (Florence, 1957). See also Bertrand Gille, *Engineers of the Renaissance* (Cambridge, Mass., 1964) and William B. Parsons, *Engineers and Engineering in the Renaissance* (Baltimore, 1939). Much material may be found in *Histoire générale des techniques*, ed. Maurice Daumas, Vols. I and II (Paris, 1962, 1965), and in *A History of Technology*, ed. Charles Singer, Vols. II and III (Oxford, 1956-57), although the latter is very irregular in quality. Franz M. Feldhaus, *Die Technik der Vorzeit, der geschichtlichen Zeit und der Naturvölker* (Leipzig, 1914), although old, remains useful over a surprising range of topics. Carlo M. Cipolla, *Guns and Sails in the Early Phase of European Expansion, 1400-1700* (London, 1966) and *Clocks and Culture, 1300-1700* (London, 1967) admirably relates technological with general history. For a study of the mid-fifteenth century enthusiasm for technology, see Lynn White, jr., "The Iconography of Temperancia and the Virtuousness of Technology," in *Action and Conviction in Early Modern Europe: Essays in Memory of E. Harris Harbison*, ed. T. K. Rabb and J. E. Seigel (Princeton, 1968).

Hieroglyphics in the Early Renaissance

A student who seeks authoritative information about the Renaissance will turn to such older classics as Burckhardt, Voigt, and perhaps Symonds; he may want to turn to such modern works as Denys Hay's *The Italian Renaissance*, 1961; or Peter Laven's *Renaissance Italy*, 1966; or to such cooperative efforts as *The Renaissance Image of Man and the World*, edited by Bernard O'Kelly, 1966; or *Aspects of the Renaissance*, edited by Archibald R. Lewis, 1967; or *The Age of the Renaissance*, edited by D. Hay, 1967. If he is especially interested in the arts of the Renaissance, there is Woelfflin's "classic" *Classic Art* for him to peruse, and there are many modern works such as Chastel's *Italian Art*, 1963; Peter and Linda Murray's *The Art of the Renaissance*, of the same year; and, above all, Panofsky's *Renaissance and Renascences*, 1960. In none of these works and many more which must remain unmentioned is there a word about Egypt. Our concept of the Renaissance is so entirely tied up with the history of Western traditions, classical above all as well as medieval, that Egypt has no place within these well-tested and — I am tempted to say — well-worn patterns of thought and investigation. But this does not mean that the problem has been overlooked in the past. On the contrary, there exists a learned and critical literature on Egypt and the Renaissance, excellent investigations made by historians of philosophy, of ideas, of magic, and of art. What I claim is that this literature has been almost entirely neglected by those who concern themselves with an integrated historical picture of the Renaissance. For the following remarks I have made ample use of the pioneering works by Karl Giehlow and Ludwig Volkmann and also of many later studies by such scholars as George Boas, Frances Yates, Paul Oskar Kristeller, Mario Praz, William Heckscher, Erik Iversen, and many others.[1]

In this paper I am concerned with hieroglyphics in the early Renaissance. To understand and assess their meaning and importance for the men of the Renaissance we have to reconstruct the intellectual climate in which they thrived.

But first I have to mention that a knowledge of Egypt reached the fifteenth century along several roads of transmission. After the Battle of Actium, in 31 B.C., Egypt became part of the Roman Empire, and the art and thought of that ancient country of mysterious wisdom immediately aroused Roman interest and admiration. The cult of Isis and Osiris gained a firm foothold in Italy.[2] Large Isis temples were built in the very center of Rome and movable objects reached Rome in a steady stream. Even obelisks were ferried across the sea — an almost unbelievable feat of engineering if you consider that the largest of these granite shafts weighed many hundred tons. In the course of time Rome had more than forty-two obelisks, twelve of which survive to this day.[3]

The last and tallest of all was shipped over by Emperor Constantius in 357. It now stands in the Piazza San Giovanni in Laterano.

Eventually most of the obelisks shared the fate of the ancient city and her treasures and were buried deep in Roman soil. But the Vatican obelisk survived in position and enjoyed enormous fame during the Middle Ages and the Renaissance as Caesar's reputed tomb. Nobody interfered with this obelisk standing next to the old basilica of Saint Peter's, the center of Christianity. Moreover, suddenly, in the late thirteenth century the most characteristic Egyptian conceptions reentered visual consciousness. Pyramids appeared in the mosaics of San Marco in Venice as Joseph's granaries (fig.1); this concept goes back

Figure 1.
Joseph's Granaries.
Detail from thirteenth-century mosaic,
San Marco, Venice.

Figure 2.
Tomb of Rolando de' Passeggeri. Ca. 1300,
Piazza San Domenico, Bologna.

to Gregory of Nazianzus.[4] And, around 1300, pyramids were for the first time incorporated in Christian tomb monuments in Bologna (fig.2).[5] Somewhat earlier, sphinxes turned up in stylistically remarkably correct adaptations in and near Rome: a particularly attractive specimen, signed by Fra Pasquale and dated 1286, is now in the museum at Viterbo (fig. 3).[6]

Figure 3.
Sphinx. By Fra Pasquali, 1286,
Museo Civico, Viterbo.

Another road of transmission of Egyptian material was due to the *Physiologus*, that strange collection of moralized and allegorized animal stories compiled in Alexandria in the first centuries of our era.[7] Many traditions, Greek, oriental, native Egyptian, were here united, and those unfamiliar with this kind of literary production may find the work weird and abstruse. People of the Middle Ages and the Renaissance thought otherwise. E. P. Evans, the author of a work on animal symbolism, rightly says that "perhaps no book except the Bible has ever been so widely diffused among so many people and for so many centuries as the *Physiologus*."[8] It was translated into every conceivable language, including Icelandic, and from the twelfth century onward it got a new lease of life through the bestiaries, the repositories of medieval zoological knowledge. *Physiologus* material reached the Renaissance in a broad stream and merged with the newly awakened interest in hieroglyphics. It is well known that Leonardo was much attracted by animal stories in moral allegorical dress.[9]

The thirteenth-century Egyptian revival was of comparatively brief duration. When the Egyptian paraphernalia — obelisks, sphinxes, pyramids — reappeared once again in the fifteenth century, they had come to stay. They formed part of an Egyptian renascence, the nature of which can only be understood by considering yet another road of transmission, namely, late antique literature. I need hardly remind you that Marsilio Ficino's most cherished concept was the reconciliation of Plato with Christ. And behind Plato there was the teaching of Moses and other ancient wisdom, a pristine theology, testified to by the Orphic Hymns, the Chaldean Oracles (which were attributed to Zoroaster), the Sibylline Oracles, and above all the Hermetica. This work by Egyptian Neoplatonists of the first centuries of our era was attributed to an Egyptian sage of remote antiquity, who had been given the name Hermes Trismegistus — the "Thrice-Greatest" — at an early time.[10] Hermes Trismegistus was also believed to have been the inventor of the art of writing, i.e., of hieroglyphs. Alexandrian Neoplatonism had combined all the esoteric oriental traditions into one philosophical edifice with the aid of allegory. What Ficino and his contemporaries attempted after the mid-fifteenth century was something similar. They did not want to dethrone Christianity, but rather show that Plato and the pre-Christian revelations attested to the truth of Christianity by way of veiled mysteries. Next to Ficino, many others (for instance Pico della Mirandola in *Heptaplus*, his commentary on the first chapter of Genesis, published in 1489) maintained that Moses and the Greeks had derived their wisdom from the Egyptians. Thus there seemed to be no doubt that the Egyptians had a mysterious knowledge of ultimate truth.

In what visual form is ultimate truth revealed? Plotinus, whom Ficino himself had translated, had given the answer. In a passage in the Fifth Book of the *Enneads*, Plotinus had said, "The Egyptian sages . . . drew pictures and carved one picture for each thing in their temples, thus making manifest the description of that thing. Thus each picture was a kind of understanding and wisdom and substance and given all at once, and not discursive reasoning and deliberation,"[11] to which Ficino added the following gloss, "The Egyptian Priests did not use individual letters to signify mysteries, but whole images of plants, trees and animals; because God has knowledge of things *not* through a multiplicity of thought processes, but rather as a simple and firm form of the thing." And he gives as an example the image of Time, painted as a winged serpent biting its tail, and concludes, "The Egyptians presented the whole of the discursive argument as it were in one complete image." In other words, in Ficino's exposition the image does not simply represent the concept — it embodies it.[12]

If one could only decipher hieroglyphs, one would have access not only to many ancient mysteries, but above all to the secret of how to express the essence of an idea, its platonic form, as it were, perfect and complete in itself, by means of an image. So the humanists of the fifteenth century turned for enlightenment to the ancient writers. There existed a fairly substantial literature from Herodotus (in the fifth century B.C.) to Ammianus Marcellinus (in the fourth century A.D.), and most of the ancient writers contained the same message, namely, that hieroglyphs adumbrated general truth in symbolic or allegorical form. In this the classical writers were, of course, absolutely wrong: they projected into hieroglyphic writing their own Hellenic mode of interpretation. Late classical authors had no idea that hieroglyphic writing was ideographic and phonetic. But they were not entirely wrong in maintaining that hieroglyphic writing was sacred in Egypt and known only to the priests: this was in fact the situation in late Egyptian history when Egypt was under foreign rule and the priests of the old religion monopolized the knowledge of hieroglyphs as a jealously guarded secret.[13]

The humanists learned from their sources — Pliny, Lucanus, Apuleius, Plutarch, Lucian, Diodorus Siculus, Clement of Alexandria, Eusebius, Iamblichus, Ammianus

Marcellinus, Macrobius, and others — that hieroglyphs contained a secret code. Moreover, from Pliny they learned that the obelisks, above all, displayed ancient Egyptian wisdom and philosophy; from Plutarch that Greek philosophers had gone to Egypt to study the mystic teachings of old; and from Clement of Alexandria that "the mysteries of the word are not to be expounded to the profane" and that "all things that shine through a veil show the truth grander and more impressive." This message, too, the initiate of the Renaissance took to heart.

The code was unexpectedly broken — or so it seemed. Shortly after 1419 the Florentine priest, Christophorus de' Buondelmonti, brought a Greek manuscript of Horapollo's *Hieroglyphica* back to Florence from a journey to Greece. Buondelmonti, probably unaware of the importance of his find, handed it to his friend Poggio Bracciolini, who had translated Diodorus Siculus and had discovered a manuscript of Ammianus Marcellinus in Germany. Niccolo de' Niccoli, it seems, also became involved. According to Ciriaco da Ancona, who sent Niccoli a hieroglyphic inscription from his Egyptian journey in 1435, no one was more interested in these matters than Niccoli.[14]

Here we are not concerned with philological problems; to us it does not matter whether or not a writer by the name of Horapollo ever existed, or whether the work was originally written in Greek or Egyptian. Suffice it to say that the compilation going under Horapollo's name is now usually dated in the fourth century after Christ. What matters is that when the Greek manuscript was studied in Florence it appeared to contain the answer to the Egyptian riddle, for it contained no fewer than 189 descriptions of hieroglyphs with their interpretations. So Horapollo soon became the standard work on hieroglyphics, and for no less than 200 years its reliability was never seriously doubted. Copies of the manuscript were circulated; Aldus in Venice printed the Greek *editio princeps* in 1505, and thirty later editions in Latin and other languages appeared in quick succession from 1515 onward. The most celebrated manuscript is the Latin translation which the Nürnberg humanist Pirckheimer handed to Emperor Maximilian in 1514 with illustrations by Dürer. At the end of the last century Giehlow found a copy of the Pirckheimer-Dürer manuscript in the Vienna Library and also a few original Dürer illustrations have been traced.

To demonstrate Horapollo's method I am showing you one of the Dürer originals, now in Berlin, with illustrations of four Horapollo hieroglyphs (fig. 4). *Top,* the hieroglyph of a dog with a stole. Horapollo's commentary reads, "If they wanted to express a most excellent prince, they painted a dog decorated with a stole, because when this animal enters temples it gazes intently upon the images of the gods. In ancient times judges also contemplated the king cloaked only with the stole (i.e., the royal robe)." Thus the hieroglyph means both prince and judge. *Above right,* the man sitting on a stool. Horapollo's text: "When they wish to indicate a shrine-bearer, they draw a house-guard, because by him is the temple guarded." *Below left,* the horoscopist. Horapollo: "To denote a horoscopist, they draw a man eating the hours." *Bottom,* fire and water. Horapollo: "To depict purity, they draw fire and water. For through these elements are all things purified."[15]

Figure 4.
Illustrations for Horapollo. By Albrecht Dürer,
Print Room, Staatliche Museen, Berlin.

I mention a few other Horapollo hieroglyphs: an ibis denotes the heart; the forequarters of a lion, strength; feet walking on water or a man without a head walking, the impossible; a bundle of papyri, ancient descent; a stork, someone who returns thanks to his parents in their old age; and so forth.

Characteristically, Dürer's illustrations to Horapollo are drawn in contemporary style; there is no attempt to imitate Egyptian stylistic characteristics. In spite of a growing taste for things Egyptian between the fifteenth and eighteenth centuries we hardly ever encounter stylistic principles even faintly reminiscent of those of the Egyptians. Egypt's influence makes itself felt on the conceptual side of artistic creation and not on the style of this long period.

From the mid-fifteenth century onwards one comes across revealing discussions of hieroglyphs. The great Alberti had, of course, given these matters much thought and incorporated an important passage in the Eighth Book of his *Ten Books on Architecture*, which I quote from Leoni's eighteenth-century translation:

The Egyptians employed symbols in the following manner: they carved an eye, by which they understood God; a vulture for Nature; a Bee for King; a circle for Time; an ox for Peace, and the like. And their reason for expressing their sense by these symbols was, that words were understood only by the respective nations that talked the language, and therefore inscriptions in common characters must in a short time be lost: as it has actually happened to our Etruscan characters: for among the ruins of several towns, castles and burial-places I have seen tombstones dug up with inscriptions on them . . . in Etruscan characters which . . . nobody can understand. And the same, the Egyptians supposed, must be the case with all sorts of writing whatsoever;

but the manner of expressing their sense which they used upon these occasions, by symbols, they thought must always be understood by learned men of all nations, to whom alone they were of the opinion that things of moment were fit to be communicated.[16]

Alberti continues and explains just how this Egyptian method was used and adapted by other nations. "Our Romans," he writes, "recorded the exploits of their great men, by carving their story in marble. This gave rise to columns, triumphal arches, porticoes enriched with memorable events preserved both in painting and sculpture."

Less revealing is what Filarete has to say in his *Treatise on Architecture*, composed in Milan between 1461 and 1464. In his Twelfth Book discussing Roman theaters he mentions the obelisk in the center "all carved with Egyptian letters." I quote from John Spencer's recent translation:

Tell me what these letters said — I do not know how to tell you, because they cannot be translated. They are all picture-letters [*lettere figurate*]; some have one animal, some another, some have a bird, some a snake, some an owl, some [are] like a saw and some like an eye . . . some with one thing and some with another, so that there are few who can translate them. It is true that the poet Francesco Filelfo told me that some of these animals meant one thing and some another. Each one had its own meaning. The obelisk means envy. . . . For the present there is not enough time to tell you [more] about this. I will tell you another time when we have more leisure.[17]

It is impossible to review here all the fifteenth-century utterances about hieroglyphs; they have been quite fully recorded by Giehlow and Volkmann. If the Romans had, as Alberti believed, in their own way made use of the

Egyptian language of symbols, specimens should be extant — and, indeed, they were discovered. A Roman temple frieze, now in the Capitoline Museum, but in the fifteenth century in San Lorenzo fuori le mura (fig. 5),

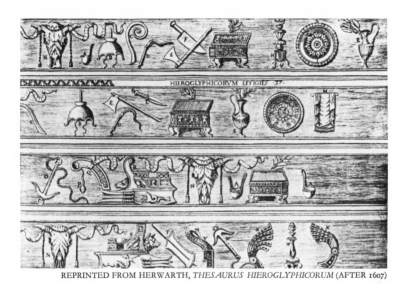

REPRINTED FROM HERWARTH, *THESAURUS HIEROGLYPHICORUM* (AFTER 1607)

Figure 5.
Roman Temple Frieze. From San Lorenzo fuori le mura,
Capitoline Museum, Rome.

was soon regarded as conveying a definite hieroglyphic message.[18] The frieze was studied and used by Mantegna (fig. 6) and other Renaissance artists and, above all, by the most gifted interpreter and inventor of hieroglyphs in Horapollo's vein, Francesco Colonna, author of the antiquarian romance *Hypnerotomachia Polifili*.

The innocent frieze in San Lorenzo with sacrificial implements stimulated Francesco Colonna to most extraordinary inventions. For instance, he describes fourteen

71

Figure 6.
Triumph of Caesar.
By Mantegna, detail from engraving by C. Huyberts.

hieroglyphs one after the other on the base of a mauso-
leum (fig. 7), illustrates them, and winds up with a co-
herent reading in Latin of their meaning which may be
translated thus, "Sacrifice your toil generously to the
God of nature. Little by little you will then subject your
soul to God, and He will take you into His firm protection, mercifully govern your life and preserve it un-
harmed."[19] Let us see how this miracle is accomplished:
the bucranium with implements means work; the eye,
God; the vulture, Nature; the altar, sacrifice; the bowl,
liberality, and so forth.

The *Hypnerotomachia* abounds with similar hieroglyphic
texts. Francesco Colonna and others were obviously convinced that they had fully recaptured the Egyptian
mysteries and that they were therefore capable of ex-

pressing themselves creatively in this language of pictorial symbols. How far removed they were from anything Egyptian needs no comment: they labored, as we have seen, under the illusion that Alexandrian Neoplatonism of late antiquity contained the true Egyptian treasure of their dreams. To this misconception we must add the strange phenomenon that, although Egyptian hieroglyphs were the starting point of their search for the lost wisdom, they never regarded it as necessary to use symbols even vaguely reminiscent of true hieroglyphs. Their interest was focused on the method rather than on the original ideogram. They applied to their own purposes what Alberti had claimed for the Romans.

Figure 7.
Hieroglyphs. From Colonna's *Hypnerotomachia*
(Venice, 1499).

73

There is a further important point to be noticed here. Colonna's hieroglyphic inscriptions expand — to borrow a phrase from Professor Edgar Wind — the symbols into an additive picture-script, whose parts had to be read like words and sentences of a discursive language. Wind also pointed out that Erasmus in the *Adagia* observed that the content of hieroglyphs "presupposed in the reader a full knowledge of the properties of each animal, plant, or thing represented."[20]

Was then the concept of intuitive understanding of the hieroglyphic mysteries an irrational dream? I do not think so. Since the symbols expressed by hieroglyphs were — in the opinion of Renaissance thinkers — reconcilable with the hidden meanings of classical mythology and with Hebrew and Christian revelation,[21] the elect few were thought capable of the immediacy of heightened experience. I think the Renaissance medal must be interpreted in this light. There is no doubt that the Renaissance medal was an important vehicle for the communication of esoteric pictographs. Medals commemorate the qualities and deeds of great men, of rulers, condottieri, and scholars. They were made for a small circle, and the ideas expressed by them were meant to remain dark and mysterious to the public at large. They were a kind of priestly currency, the reserve of the few — just as in their view the Egyptian hieroglyphs had been the secret of the sacerdotal caste.

In a medallion usually regarded as a self-portrait of Alberti (fig. 8), probably dating from 1438, there appears a winged eye in the space under the chin. The same emblem is shown on the reverse of Matteo de' Pasti's medal of Alberti (fig. 9), dating about ten years later.[22]

74

In this medal the eye is surrounded by a laurel wreath, and under it appears the motto taken from Cicero, *Quid Tum* — "What Then?" Alberti himself described, as has recently been shown,[23] the winged eye and its sym-

Figure 8.
Medallion, Self-Portrait. By L. B. Alberti, 1438.

Figure 9.
Medal of L. B. Alberti (obverse and reverse). By Matteo de' Pasti.

bolism in his dialogue *Anuli*. He describes the wreath as the symbol of joy and glory and the eye both as a symbol of God's omniscience and as a reminder to be wide awake, all-embracing as far as the power of our intelligence allows. Whether or not the motto What Then was meant to refer to afterdeath and thus to the readiness to appear before God's judgment (as some interpreters have wanted) may be left undecided.

The greatest medallist of the quattrocento and probably of all time, Pisanello, gives a good measure of the close interweaving of the medieval and the hieroglyphic traditions. My first example is a fairly late medal, the reverse of the medal of Alfonso v, king of Aragon and Sicily, of 1449 (fig. 10), which shows an eagle perched on a tree stump with a dead fawn; around the eagle are other birds of prey and the inscription *Liberalitas Augusta*.[24] The image is meant to symbolize the king's liberality. The source for the story is not Horapollo but Pliny. From here it was taken over by medieval writers such as Bartholomaeus

76

Figure 10.
Medal of King Alfonso V (reverse).
By Pisanello, 1449.

Anglicanus and Albertus Magnus. It spread into other late medieval material, especially the *Fiori di Virtù* (fig. 11), a well-known Tuscan text of moralizing animal stories, of which a number of fourteenth- and fifteenth-century manuscripts are preserved.[25] Leonardo must have owned a copy of the *Fiori di Virtù* and copied from it the comment to the eagle image: "Of the eagle men say that he has never so great hunger as not to leave part of his prey to those birds which are around him."[26] We may assume

77

Figure 11.
The Eagle and his Prey. From a manuscript of *Fiori di Virtù*,
Florence, Bibl. Riccardiana, cod. 1711, fol. 21,
ca. 1450.

that Pisanello too was stimulated for his image by the
Fiori di Virtù.

Similarly, an earlier hieroglyphic medal by Pisanello,
that of the scholar Belloto Cumano of 1447 with an
ermine on the reverse (fig. 12), ultimately derives from
Pliny.[27] Based on Pliny's story, the ermine became an
often used symbol of purity and was also incorporated
as such in the *Fiori di Virtù*, and once again Leonardo
used it. It appears prominently in his Portrait of a Woman
(Cracow) whom some scholars have — in my view correctly — regarded to be the portrait of Cecilia Gallerani
(fig. 13), dating from about 1483.

Cecilia was the mistress of Lodovico il Moro, and
Lodovico used the ermine as his personal emblem. But
there is more to it. Ermine in Greek is γαλῆ or γαλέη and

there is therefore here a punning reference to Gallerani, the name of the sitter.[28] In addition, the animal symbolizes the sitter's virtue. Although the ermine does not form part of Horapollo's catalogue of hieroglyphs, the spirit that informs this allegorical portrait fully accords with the hieroglyphic mode of thought. Moreover, we may safely infer that people at Lodovico il Moro's court were expected to understand in a flash all the subtle implications incorporated into the picture. A discursive

Figure 12.
Medal of Belloto Cumano (reverse). By Pisanello, 1447.

79

Figure 13.
Portrait of Cecilia Gallerani. By Leonardo da Vinci, ca. 1483,
Czartoryski Museum, Cracow.

decipherment kills the immediacy of effect of the image.

The salamander had — as you will recall — a very long symbolical lease of life. According to Aristotle the salamander had the power of extinguishing fire,[29] and through the *Physiologus* and the bestiaries the legend was disseminated in Christian Europe. In Christian allegorical thought the salamander typifies the righteous man who is

Figure 14.
Medal of Antonio Spannocchi (obverse and reverse).
By Francesco di Giorgio.

Figure 15.
Medal of Doge Battista II (obverse and reverse).
By Battista Elia of Genoa (?).

81

not consumed by the fire of luxury and lust.[30] Salamanders
are common on medals and here they symbolize new
shades of meaning. Francesco di Giorgio's medal of
Antonio Spannocchi (fig. 14), member of the Sienese
merchant-banker family, shows on the reverse a salamander and the legend: *Ignis ipsam Recreat et me Cruciat*[31]—
"Fire Invigorates Him [the salamander] but Torments

Figure 16.
Top left, Bulls Adoring a Picture of the Virgin;
top right, Bulls Kneeling before the Cross;
bottom, Bulls Adoring the Portrait of Pope Alexander VI.
By Pinturicchio,
Apartamento Borgia,
Vatican.

82

Me": probably a reference to the flames and torments of love.

A medal attributed to Battista Elia of Genoa with the Doge Battista II Campofregoso (1478-83) on the obverse, shows on the reverse the Egyptian bird trochilus flying into the jaws of a crocodile (fig. 15) and the motto: *Peculiares Audacia et Victus*.[32] Herodotus (II, 68), Pliny, Solinus, and others had commented on the habits of the trochilus, which feeds by picking crumbs from the teeth of sleeping crocodiles, and this story was incorporated into the *Physiologus*. As the motto implying sustenance through extraordinary boldness indicates, the medal celebrates some daring and dangerous action on the Doge's part and a further study of his life would probably make it possible to pinpoint the occasion. What is of interest here is that both the hieroglyphic and the *Physiologus* traditions were used for precisely the same purpose, namely, to convey a generally valid concept by means of a pictograph.

I am concerned with this medal for yet another reason. Doge Campofregoso's advisor was that strange scholar Fra Giovanni Nanni da Viterbo who later held office at the Roman Curia and became advisor to the Borgia Pope Alexander VI. Nanni has won fame for his forgeries of Egyptian, Chaldean, Greek, and Latin texts, first published about 1498 in *Antiquitatum variarum volumina XVII*, forgeries designed to prove the close connection between the primeval wisdom of the Egyptians and that of the Romans. There can be little doubt that Nanni da Viterbo was responsible (as has been surmised by Giehlow and Saxl)[33] for constructing a genealogical link between the Apis bull and the Borgia family, that he — in short — devised the program for Pinturicchio's frescoes in the Apartamento Borgia in the Vatican where the story of Isis and Osiris is represented; the murder of Osiris; his reincarnation as the Apis bull; and the Christianized Apis who adores the Cross, the Virgin, and the Vicar of Christ (fig. 16).

Nanni's wild imagination bore other, similar fruit. He maintained that Osiris had come to Italy accompanied by his son Hercules Aegyptius. The German Emperor Maximilian, who was steeped in hieroglyphics, emblematics, and astrology, regarded Nanni's discovery as a useful lead to his own genealogy, which his court humanists traced through Hercules Aegyptius and Osiris back to Noah.[34]

I cannot forego the temptation to say a few words about the greatest hieroglyphic monument, Dürer's *Triumphal Arch of Maximilian*, the cooperative effort of many minds and hands and the largest woodcut ever created: it measures $11\frac{1}{2}$ by $9\frac{3}{4}$ feet and consists of no less than 192 separate blocks. The famous crowning feature in the central register shows the emperor enthroned and surrounded by symbolic animals — all gleaned from Horapollo (fig. 17). The court historiographer Stabius's German and Pirckheimer's Latin texts allow us to decode the message conveyed by the image. I quote from Panofsky's excellent English translation (the interpolations are Panofsky's):

Maximilian [the Emperor himself] — a prince [dog draped with stole] of great piety [star above the Emperor's crown], most magnanimous, powerful and courageous [lion], ennobled by imperishable and eternal fame [basilisk on the Emperor's crown], descending from ancient lineage [the sheaf of papyrus on which he is seated], Roman Emperor [eagles embroidered in the cloth of honor], endowed with all the gifts of nature and possessed of art and learning [dew descending from the sky] and master of a great part of the terrestrial globe [snake encircling the scepter] — has with warlike virtue and great discretion [bull] won a shining victory [falcon on the orb] over the mighty king here indicated [cock on a serpent, meaning the King of France], and thereby watchfully protected himself [crane raising its foot] from the stratagems of said enemy, which has been deemed impossible [feet walking through water by themselves] by all mankind.[35]

Through Emperor Maximilian's humanist circle hieroglyphics became firmly established in Germany. But I want to return to an earlier period in Italy. To what extent artists of the quattrocento accepted this language has not yet been sufficiently investigated. It is well known that Mantegna incorporated into his *Triumph of Caesar* hieroglyphs culled from the ancient frieze in San Lorenzo fuori le mura. And I think that many of the symbols carried about should also be interpreted hieroglyphically. It has been recognized, for instance, that the orb with cornucopia and rudder next to Caesar (fig. 6) is a hieroglyph signifying the affluency of the world under Caesar's stewardship.[36]

More important perhaps than such traces of hieroglyphic expression and of a direct dependence on Horapollo is the fact that there existed a broad movement intent to reconcile mythology, allegory, hieroglyphic and near-hieroglyphic concepts with Christian thought. Such interpretation should probably be applied to at least some of the grotesques, those typical Renaissance creations derived from the study of the decorations in the *Domus Aurea*.[37] A cycle of grotesques once decorated the cloisters of Santa Giustina at Padua. They are largely

Figure 17.
Hieroglyphic Image of Emperor Maximilian.
Detail from Dürer's woodcut of the *Ehrenpforte*,
1515.

destroyed, but are known from eighteenth-century engravings (figs. 18 and 19).[38] They were begun by Bernardo
Parentino for Abbot Gasparo before 1500, but were not

Figures 18 *(above)* and 19 *(over)*
Francesco Mengardi's Engravings of the Lost Fresco Decorations
in the Cloisters of Santa Giustina, Padua.

finished until the forties of the sixteenth century. According to a contemporary chronicle Gasparo had selected figures and stories of the Romans, fables from the
poets, tombs, stones with inscriptions, Egyptian emblems, and other thoughtful ideas. A late sixteenth-century work on the frescoes — now lost — bore the title:

REPRINTED FROM VOLKMANN, *BILDERSCHRIFTEN*

"Elucidation or rather copious explanation of the historical scenes and hieroglyphs painted in the Cloisters."[39] The engravings after the frescoes show that hieroglyphs from the *Hypnerotomachia* (fig. 20) played a large part in the decorations: there is the seated woman with wings in one

88

hand and a tortoise in the other (meaning, Temper Speed by Sitting Down, Inertia by Getting Up); there are the two genii who together are holding the center of the circle which surrounds them (meaning, The Fortunate Keep to the Middle Road); there are also some elephant-devouring ants at both sides of a rod with snakes, and so forth.

Hieroglyphs from Horapollo have been traced in the room adjoining Correggio's Camera di San Paolo at Parma, a room that was decorated in 1514 by Alessandro Araldi for the abbess Donna Giovanna da Piacenza, namely, the snake biting its tail and the feet walking through water.[40] These hieroglyphs appear in the company of exemplars from mythology and of biblical scenes. The adjoining room, decorated by Correggio between 1518 and 1519, has been fully investigated by Panofsky,[41]

Figure 20.
Hieroglyphs. From Colonna's *Hypnerotomachia*.

89

and those who know his book will agree that I cannot attempt to add to it. Only one brief comment: as is well known, for his decoration Correggio drew heavily on classical coins, just as the artists of medals did. Moreover, as Panofsky's analysis has revealed, he expressed through classical images ideas, cryptic allusions, mysteries accessible only to the learned and initiate. Correggio's language in this room is implicitly, though not explicitly, hieroglyphic, and it is revealing that a number of the images he used also appear later in Piero Valeriano's *Hieroglyphica* (1556).

In support of my contention that hieroglyphics and the broad stream of Renaissance allegory and symbolism merge, a good deal of early literary evidence can be adduced. For instance, Poliziano's pupil, Pietro Crinito (born in 1465), who wrote a work with the title "On the hieroglyphs of the Egyptians," now unfortunately lost, in his *De honesta disciplina* of 1504 made the point that there is no difference between hieroglyphs and symbols.[42] He also agreed with Pico della Mirandola and others that the Old Testament was written in allegorical language, and the study of the twelfth-century Byzantine writer Tzetzes convinced him that Homer also contained hieroglyphic mysteries.

Ficino himself closed the gap between Egyptian and Christian symbols by stating that for the Egyptians the cross signified afterlife and that they incised it on the chest of figures of Serapis. Filippo Fasanini, who translated Horapollo into Latin (Bologna, 1517), and who also lectured on hieroglyphics at the University of Bologna, explained that the reader can learn from his work the true nature of animals, birds, fishes, trees, and the like. To go a step further and also farther in time: Andrea Alciati, born in Milan in 1492, studied at Bologna under Fasanini and it was probably then that he conceived the idea of embedding hieroglyphs in verses. For what else is his famous collection of emblems, ready for the press in 1521, but published not until ten years later with the title *Emblematum libellus*. Following Plutarch, Alciati declared classical symbolism and hieroglyphs to be the same thing. Let us recall that Alberti had implied this thought about three generations earlier. But the great summation of hieroglyphical thought and material came a little later, in Pierio Valeriano's *Hieroglyphica* of 1556. Pierio Valeriano, whose real name was Giovan Pietro della Fosse, was born at Belluno in 1477. He was the nephew of the learned Fra Urbano Valeriano Bolzanio (ca. 1443-1524), the friend of Francesco Colonna (author of the *Hypnerotomachia*), the center of a circle of Venetian scholars dedicated to the study of hieroglyphs and the tutor of Giovanni Medici, later Leo X. Pierio was introduced into hieroglyphic studies by his uncle and dedicated his life's work to them. In 1509 he was in Rome, where he became private secretary to Cardinal Giulio de Medici and tutor to Ippolito de Medici. His *Hieroglyphica* is a vast compilation for which he equally used Horapollo, the *Physiologus*, Greek and Roman material, the Cabala, and the Bible. In this way he was implementing what had been done for a hundred years, and his point of view is clearly expressed in his dedicatory remark that "to speak hieroglyphically is nothing else but to disclose the [true] nature of things divine and human."[43] It is also worth noting that he refers to the efforts made in this field of study by Poliziano, Crinito, and Filippo Beroaldo,[44] who had published in

1500 a learned commentary to Apuleius's *Golden Ass* with important remarks on hieroglyphics.

The guidance provided by Valeriano to seekers of truth is best illustrated by the fact that a large number of editions of the work became necessary — no less than eleven in the next seventy years. Valeriano had in fact an enormous following, but to discuss this topic would mean trespassing on the chronological limits set by this conference. Let me only assert that, while Valeriano did not contribute any revolutionary ideas to our problem, he was instrumental in transforming a philosophy of hieroglyphics into a philological discipline. Nevertheless he takes us back to the beginnings, and that means to Florence. Vasari tells us that Pierio was his teacher in Latin and other erudite subjects.[45] Appropriately the *Hieroglyphica* is dedicated to Duke Cosimo de Medici, and in the dedication we read: " 'I will open my mouth in a parable; I will utter dark sayings of old' (Psalm 78:2). What else did He want to say than that His language be hieroglyphic and He voice the ancient records allegorically."[46]

BY RUDOLF WITTKOWER

NOTES

1. The most important bibliographical references may be given here. Karl Giehlow, "Die Hieroglyphenkunde des Humanismus in der Allegorie der Renaissance," *Jahrbuch der Kunsthistorischen Sammlungen des Allerhöchsten Kaiserhauses* (1915), XXXII, 1-218, the masterpiece *hors concours*, remains the basis for all later studies of hieroglyphics in the Renaissance. Ludwig Volkmann, *Bilderschriften der Renaissance: Hieroglyphik und Emblematik in ihren Beziehungen und Fortwirkungen* (Leipzig, 1923), is a brilliant summary of Giehlow's work. George Boas, *The Hieroglyphics of Horapollo* (New York, 1950), is a translation of Horapollo's text with an excellent introduction. Erik Iversen, *The Myth of Egypt and its Hieroglyphics in European Tradition* (Copenhagen, 1961), written by an Egyptologist, lucidly covers a vast panorama and has been very helpful to me. The most recent book on Egypt in Europe, Jurgis Baltrušaitis, *La Quête d'Isis: Introduction à l'Egyptomanie* (Paris, 1967), contains much interesting material, but yielded little for the purpose of this paper.

2. See Franz Cumont, *The Oriental Religions in Roman Paganism* (New York, 1956).

3. E. Nash, "Obelisk und Circus," *Mitteilungen des Deutschen Archaeologischen Institutes, Römische Abteilung*, LXIV (1957), 232-59, contains a reliable account of all the obelisks standing in Rome today. Neither Cesare D'Onofrio's *Gli obelischi di Roma* (Rome, 1965), nor Erik Iversen's *Obelisks in Exile* (Copenhagen, 1968) was available to me when the manuscript was completed.

4. Iversen, *The Myth of Egypt*, pp. 59, 153, cites also other sources.

5. The free-standing tombs showing the sarcophagus on a platform carried by columns and protected by a pyramid roof were erected to professors of the university and high-ranking citizens; early examples near San Francesco are Accursio (d. 1260), Odofredo (d. 1265), Rolandino de'Romanzi (d. 1284); the more famous later ones near San Domenico are Egidio Foscherari (d. 1289) and Rolandino de'Passeggeri (d. 1296).

6. So far as I can see, the Egyptian revival of the thirteenth century has never been given the attention it would deserve. To a considerable extent it is connected with the Cosmati Vasselletto, father and son, who left works of Egyptian inspiration in the cloisters of San Giovanni in Laterano, at San Paolo fuori le Mura, in the cathedral at Anagni and elsewhere. For Fra Pasquale's remarkable sphinx at Viterbo, see Italo Faldi's entry, "Pasquale Romano," in Museo Civico di Viterbo, *Dipinti e sculture dal medioevo al XVIII secolo* (Viterbo, 1955), pp. 54-55, with bibliography.

7. The classic edition is still that by Friedrich Lauchert, *Geschichte des Physiologus* (Strassburg, 1889).

8. E. P. Evans, *Animal Symbolism in Ecclesiastical Architecture* (London, 1896), p. 62.

9. Jean Paul Richter, ed., *The Literary Works of Leonardo da Vinci*, 2nd ed., rev.

by Jean Paul and Irma A. Richter (London and New York, 1939), II, 259, has surveyed the sources for Leonardo's observations on animals.

10. For those unfamiliar with the hermetic tradition, I cannot do better than recommend the first chapter ("Hermes Trismegistus") in Frances A. Yates's brilliant book *Giordano Bruno and the Hermetic Tradition* (Chicago, 1964).

11. Quoted from Boas, *The Hieroglyphics of Horapollo*, p. 22.

12. For this and the following citation I am indebted to E. H. Gombrich, "*Icones Symbolicae:* The Visual Image in Neo-Platonic Thought," *Journal of the Warburg and Courtauld Institutes*, XI (1948), 172. Cf. Boas, p. 28. Edgar Wind, *Pagan Mysteries in the Renaissance*, 2nd ed. (London, 1968), pp. 206-8, turns against what he regards as unsupported speculations concerning "a positive theory of optical intuition" in Neoplatonic thought.

13. For a full discussion of the material presented in this and the following paragraph, see the first two chapters of Iversen's book, cited above.

14. Volkmann, *Bilderschriften der Renaissance*, p. 9.

15. Boas, p. 78.

16. Bk. VIII, chap. iv. I have changed a few words where the translation did not seem adequate.

17. Filarete's *Treatise on Architecture*, trans. John R. Spencer (New Haven and London, 1965), I, 152. The passage clearly shows that Filarete's knowledge of hieroglyphics was scanty, one is inclined to think, because he moved at the fringe of the intellectual elite.

18. See Volkmann, pp. 16f; Iversen, pp. 66f.

19. I am following Iversen's translation, p. 68. An influence of the San Lorenzo frieze on Francesco Colonna has always been maintained since first propounded by Christian Huelsen, "Le illustrazioni della *Hypnerotomachia Polifili* e la antichità di Roma," *La Bibliofilia*, XII (1910-11), 165, but more recently Italian scholars have declined to accept it; see M. T. Casella and Giovanni Pozzi, *Francesco Colonna: Biografia e opere* (Padua, 1959), II, 54 f., and Francesco Colonna, *Hypnerotomachia Poliphili*. Edizione critica e commento a cura di Giovanni Pozzi e Lucia A. Ciapponi (Padua, 1964), II, 68f., with a valuable analysis of each "hieroglyph" used by Colonna in our example.

20. Wind, *Pagan Mysteries*, p. 208, n. 58.

21. See Frances A. Yates, *The French Academies of the Sixteenth Century* (London, 1947), pp. 131f.

22. On these medals, see G. F. Hill, *A Corpus of Italian Medals of the Renaissance before Cellini* (London, 1930), Nos. 16-18, 161.

23. R. Watkins, "L. B. Alberti's Emblem, The Winged Eye, and his Name, Leo," *Mitteilungen des Kunsthistorischen Institutes in Florenz*, IX (1959-60), 256-58.

24. Hill, *Italian Medals before Cellini*, No. 41.

25. O. Lehmann-Brockhaus, "Tierdarstellungen der *Fiori di Virtù*," in *Mitteilungen des Kunsthistorischen Institutes in Florenz*, VI (1940-41), 5ff., 11.

26. Richter, *Literary Works of Leonardo da Vinci,* II, 262, No. 1225. For, Leonardo's quotations from the *Fiori di Virtù,* see Richter, 260-65, 276, II, 366, Nos. 1220-34, 1263, 1264, 1469.

27. Hill, No. 39.

28. The picture was in the collection of Prince Czartoryski and is now in the museum of the same name. The often debated question of the authenticity of this picture was left undecided in the latest authoritative monograph on Leonardo: Ludwig Heinrich Heydenreich, *Leonardo da Vinci* (London and New York, 1954), p. 35. In the most thorough investigation of the picture, E. Möller, "Leonardo da Vinci's Bildnis der Cecilia Gallerani in der Gallerie des Fürsten Czartoryski in Krakau," *Monatshefte für Kunstwissenschaft,* IX (1916), 313-36, came out very strongly on the side of authenticity without even knowing the Greek reference which, to my mind, clinches the issue. This important discovery is hidden in an out-of-place footnote by the Editor of the *Burlington Magazine,* X (1906-7), 310, but was known and used by Sir Kenneth Clark, *Leonardo da Vinci,* rev. ed. (Baltimore, Md., 1959), p. 54.

29. *Hist. an.,* V, 552 b.

30. See R. Wittkower, "Marco Polo and the Pictorial Tradition of the Marvels of the East," in Istituto Italiano per il medio ed estremo oriente, *Oriente Poliano* (Rome, 1957), p. 161. For further material on the salamander's qualities, see Robert A. Koch, "The Salamander in Van der Goes' Garden of Eden," *Journal of the Warburg and Courtauld Institutes,* XXVIII (1965), 323-26.

31. Hill, No. 314.

32. Hill, No. 728.

33. Giehlow, *Jahrbuch,* pp. 44ff.; F. Saxl, *Lectures* (London, 1957), I, 186f. For Nanni da Viterbo see also Volkmann, p. 12, and passim, and Iversen, pp. 62f.

34. Maximilian was immensely interested in the genealogy of his house. The rich surviving material was assembled in Vienna on the occasion of the Maximilian exhibition; see Vienna Nationalbibliothek, *Maximilian I, 1459-1519: Ausstellung* (Vienna, 1959), pp. 51-62, esp. Nos. 183-202, with additional bibliography.

35. Erwin Panofsky, *Albrecht Dürer* (Princeton, N.J., 1943), p. 177.

36. For Bramante's active involvement in hieroglyphics, see E. H. Gombrich, "Hypnerotomochiana," *Journal of the Warburg and Courtauld Institutes,* XIV (1951), 119-22, and Peter Murray, " 'Bramante Milanese': the Printings and Engravings," *Arte Lombarda,* VII (1962), 31f. To quote some later examples: Sebastiano del Piombo's Portrait of Andrea Doria in the collection of Prince Doria Pamphili, Rome, dated 1526, has a parapet on which six "hieroglyphs" selected from the San Lorenzo fuori le mura frieze are assembled. Similar hieroglyphs appear in Giulio Romano's apse fresco of the Assumption of the Virgin in the Cathedral at Verona (1534), in the frieze under the painted balustrade; see Frederick Hart, *Giulio Romano* (New Haven, 1958), II, fig. 429.

37. See J. Schulz, "Pinturicchio and the Revival of Antiquity," *Journal of the Warburg and Courtauld Institutes*, XXV (1962), 47ff., with additional bibliography.

38. For more detailed information about these frescoes, see Léon Dorez, "Des origines et de la diffusion du 'Songe de Poliphile,'" *Revue des Bibliothèques*, VI (1896), 243-66; Giehlow, pp. 70-73, and Volkmann, pp. 23-26.

39. *Elucidario o sia copiosa spiegazione delle figure istoriche e geroglifici del Chiostro dipinto;* see Volkmann, p. 23.

40. Guy de Tervarent, *Attributs et symboles dans l'art profane, 1450-1600* (Geneva, 1958), cols. 307, 347.

41. Erwin Panofsky, *The Iconography of Corregio's Camera di San Paolo* (London, 1961).

42. For this and the following, see Giehlow, pp. 83-88, and Volkmann, p. 28.

43. See Iversen, p. 73.

44. In the edition of the *Hieroglyphica* at my disposal: Lyons, 1626, fol. 3^r.

45. Wolfgang Kallab, *Vasaristudien, Quellenschriften für Kunstgeschichte und Kunsttechnik des Mittelalters und der Neuzeit*, n.s., XV (Vienna and Leipzig, 1908), 13, 21-24.

46. Valeriano, *ed. cit.*, fol. 3r: " 'Aperiam in parabolis os meum, & in aenigmate antiqua loquar', quid aliud sibi voluit, quam hieroglyphice, sermonem faciam & allegorice vetusta rerum proferam monumenta?" Both Volkmann, p. 36, and Wind, p. 13, n. 43, have referred to this important passage.

SELECTIVE BIBLIOGRAPHY

Alberti, Leone Battisti. *Ten Books of Architecture,* trans. James Leoni. London, 1726.

Baltrušaitis, Jurgis. *La Quête d'Isis: Introduction à l'Égyptomanie.* Paris, 1967.

Casella, M. T., and Giovanni Pozzi. *Francesco Colonna: Biografia e opere.* 2 vols. Padua, 1959.

Cumont, Franz. *The Oriental Religions in Roman Paganism.* New York, 1956.

Dorez, Léon. "Des origines et de la diffusion du 'Songe de Poliphilie,'" *Revue des Bibliothèques,* VI (1896), 239-83.

Evans, E. P. *Animal Symbolism in Ecclesiastical Architecture.* London, 1896.

Giehlow, Karl. "Die Hieroglyphenkunde des Humanismus in der Allegorie der Renaissance," *Jahrbuch der Kunsthistorischen Sammlungen des Allerhöchsten Kaiserhauses,* XXXII (1915), 1-218.

Gombrich, E. H. "Hypnerotomachiana," *Journal of the Warburg and Courtauld Institutes,* XIV (1951), 119-22.

Hart, Frederick. *Giulio Romano.* 2 vols. New Haven, 1958.

Hill, G. F. *A Corpus of Italian Medals of the Renaissance before Cellini.* 2 vols. London, 1930.

Huelsen, Christian, "Le illustrazioni della *Hypnerotomachia Polifili* e le anti-chità di Roma," *La Bibliofilia*, XII (1910-11), 161-76.

Iversen, Erik. *The Myth of Egypt and its Hieroglyphics in European Tradition.* Copenhagen, 1961.

Koch, Robert A. "The Salamander in Van der Goes' Garden of Eden," *Journal of the Warburg and Courtauld Institutes*, XXVIII (1965), 323-26.

Lauchert, Friedrich. *Geschichte des Physiologus.* Strassburg, 1889.

Lehmann-Brockhaus, O. "Tierdarstellung der *Fiori di Virtù*," *Mitteilungen des Kunsthistorischen Institutes in Florenz*, VI (1940-41), 1-32.

Murray, Peter. " 'Bramante Milanese': the Printings and Engravings," *Arte Lombarda*, VII (1962), 25-42.

Panofsky, Erwin. *Albrecht Dürer.* Princeton, N.J., 1943.

———. *The Iconography of Corregio's Camera di San Paolo.* London, 1961.

Pozzi, Giovanni, and Lucia A. Ciapponi. Ed. Francesco Colonna. *Hypnerotomachia Poliphili: Edizione critica e commento.* 2 vols. Padua, 1964.

Richter, Jean Paul, and Irma A., eds. *The Literary Works of Leonardo da Vinci.* 2nd rev. ed. 2 vols. London and New York, 1939.

Saxl, F. *Lectures.* 2 vols. London, 1957.

Schulz, J. "Pinturicchio and the Revival of Antiquity," *Journal of the Warburg and Courtauld Institutes*, XXV (1962), 35-55.

Tervarent, Guy de. *Attributs et symboles dans l'art profane, 1450-1600.* Geneva, 1958.

Valeriano, Pierio. *Hieroglyphica.* Lyons, 1626.

Vienna Nationalbibliothek. *Maximilian I, 1459-1519: Ausstellung.* Vienna, 1959.

Volkman, Ludwig. *Bilderschriften der Renaissance: Hieroglyphik und Emblematik in ihren Beziehungen und Fortwirkungen.* Leipzig, 1923.

Watkins, R. "L. B. Alberti's Emblem, The Winged Eye, and his Name, Leo," *Mitteilungen des Kunsthistorischen Institutes in Florenz*, IX (1959-60), 256-58.

Wind, Edgar. *Pagan Mysteries in the Renaissance.* 2nd ed. London, 1968.

Wittkower, R. "Marco Polo and the Pictorial Tradition of the Marvels of the East," in Istituto Italiano per il medio ed estremo oriente, *Oriente Poliano*, Rome, 1957, pp. 155-72.

Yates, Frances A. *The French Academies of the Sixteenth Century.* London, 1947.

———. *Giordano Bruno and the Hermetic Tradition.* Chicago, 1964.

The Origins of the Early Modern State

Nowadays we take the state for granted. We may grumble about its demands; we may complain about its encroachments on our liberties, but we can hardly envisage life without it. Most men find it easier to accept the tyranny of a state than to endure the agony of being stateless. When Hale wrote his *Man Without a Country* in the nineteenth century he could not begin to imagine how miserable such a man would be in the twentieth century.

As far as Europe* is concerned, this is a relatively new

---

* As the reader will soon discover, the conclusions of this paper are based almost entirely on examples drawn from French and English history. This is not to deny that other European states existed or that their history was unimportant. On the whole, however, these other states were formed later than France and England, went through many of the same experiences, and often deliberately imitated the French (or more rarely the English) model. Thus France and England are reasonably typical of the European states that survived into the modern period. The Italian city-states offer a special problem. During their brief period of brilliance they showed remarkable ingenuity; for example, they were far ahead of France and England in the fields of taxation and public finance. But their problems were different because of their small size and their urban-based economies. Their staying power was weak; overall they must be

situation. Not long ago — as historians measure time — Europeans gave their allegiance to family, neighborhood, lord, rather than to the political abstraction called the state. Social outcasts were those disowned by the family, exiled by the neighborhood, rejected by the lord. There was a strong sense of reciprocal obligation among those who knew each other personally, but this sense of obligation faded rapidly with distance. Local communities or lordships were relatively strong; kingdoms and empires were weak.

Eventually social and economic development combined with the desires of certain lords for more power and more wealth to create larger political communities which eventually became states. Europeans were not the first nor the only people to found states, but the European experience was unusual in three respects. First, the process was slow. The first political units that had some of the attributes of a state appeared about 1100; the final amalgamation of all the ingredients that make a modern state took place only in the nineteenth century. Second, the rate of development of different parts of the state apparatus was extremely uneven. In general, offices and agencies dealing with internal affairs — courts of justice, financial departments, provincial administrations — were well established by 1300. Agencies dealing with external affairs — foreign offices, war and navy departments, permanent military establishments — appeared much later and

accounted political failures. Except in diplomacy, they had little influence on the development of the trans-Alpine states. I have therefore deliberately left them out of the discussion. (An extended and revised version of this article, reprinted here with permission of the publisher, appears in *On the Medieval Origins of the Modern State*, by Joseph R. Strayer. Copyright 1970 by Princeton University Press, Princeton, New Jersey.)

can scarcely be said to have had a stable existence until the seventeenth century. Third, the theories used to justify the development and consolidation of the power of the state were highly legalistic; law made the state and the state existed to enforce the law.[1] And the law on which the state was based was not criminal law which punished offenses against the state, but civil law, which protected individual rights.

These three peculiarities in the end made the European state unusually powerful, because they enabled it to gain the cooperation and active participation of most of its subjects. Slow development meant that the demands of the state seldom exceeded the willingness of subjects to comply with those demands. In fact, in some periods of European history the state was blamed for doing too little rather than for doing too much. Early concentration on internal affairs meant that the first organs of government to develop were those which were obviously and immediately useful to a large part of the population. It is easy to see that a court of justice may protect life and property; it is somewhat less clear that a foreign office or a war department will produce the same benefits. Moreover, the organizations dealing with internal affairs had time to develop fixed and regular procedures and to gain a considerable degree of autonomy before the state became very strong. They were thus less subject to arbitrary interference by the executive than agencies dealing with foreign relations. Since the organizations concerned with internal affairs (notably the courts) were those whose activity directly affected the ordinary citizen, their relative independence from political pressures helped to generate confidence in the impartiality of the state. Finally, the emphasis on law harmonized with the religious and intellectual ideals that prevailed during the entire period of state building. God was law; the world was ruled by divine law; human law was a participation in divine law.[2] Thus a state based on law was a state which was carrying out God's plans for humanity. And if the state fell away from this high ideal, its wrongful actions could be checked by an appeal to the law — often by an appeal to the law which the state itself had made.[3]

On the other hand, while slow and uneven development had long-term advantages, it could also cause periods of crisis — periods in which the state scarcely seemed able to cope with its problems. One such period of crisis occurred in the fourteenth and fifteenth centuries, and it is that period that I want to discuss in this essay.

Let me start by reviewing what had been accomplished down to 1300. This review will not only supply some necessary background material; it will also, I hope, provide some idea of what I mean by a "state." The state is a process, not an entity which can be boxed up in a logical definition. And it is only by describing the process that one can describe a state, or a certain type of state.

In western Europe, by 1300, there were political units that had achieved stability in space and continuity in time. A king and his people no longer wandered from the Baltic to the Black Sea to the Bay of Biscay as the Goths had done in the fourth and fifth centuries. There were fluctuations on the fringes but the core area ruled by the king of the English or the king of the French had remained fixed for several centuries. In these areas of political stability, institutions had developed which were self-perpetuating. They did not depend on historical accidents — the ability of the ruler, the personal relationships among the nobles, the exhortations of religious leaders. They were accepted by everyone as necessary and permanent; they followed regular and predictable patterns of actions. As I said earlier, these institutions dealt primarily with the administration of justice, the collection of revenue, and the control of political subunits (shires, bailiwicks). Finally, the idea had been accepted that in areas of political stability and self-perpetuating institutions there was an authority which could make final decisions. These decisions were binding on all men within certain boundaries and were irreversible by any power outside those boundaries. In short, the concept of sovereignty existed even if the word did not. It was a concept that saw final appellate jurisdiction as the essential sign of sovereignty, which may be one reason why its existence has not been recognized by some political theorists. It was not that thirteenth-century kings did not legislate — they did, often on important subjects.[4] It was not that they lacked the physical power to enforce their orders, though they naturally preferred to use this power only in cases of real necessity. But legislation, though it might be important, occurred infrequently, and no thirteenth-century ruler sought a monopoly of power — it sufficed if he had greater power than any of his subjects. Thus, the real test of sovereignty was the right to give final judgment in a court of law. It was by claiming appellate jurisdiction that Philip the Fair sought to establish his authority in Aquitaine and Flanders[5] and that Edward I tried to end the independence of Scotland.[6]

Conversely, the lack of such appellate jurisdiction meant that the Holy Roman Emperor did not have sovereign power either in Italy or in Germany.

Perhaps even more important than the growth of new institutions and new political ideas was a transfer of loyalty to the state. The transfer operated to the detriment of both local authorities and the universal Church.[7] It was by no means a complete transfer — local patriotisms and devotion to the commonwealth of Christendom continued to exist. But the idea had emerged that the greatest good was the preservation of the state, and that to preserve the state subjects could be required to give up their lives and their property.[8] Even the pope admitted, grudgingly, that in an emergency kings could tax the clergy for the defense of the realm.[9]

The medieval state was perhaps most effective about the year 1300. During the next century some of the weaknesses caused by the uneven development of medieval institutions were revealed. A gap between policy makers and professional administrators appeared. Such a gap is not uncommon; it was more serious than usual in the fourteenth century because the policy makers had to deal with precisely those areas of government (foreign relations and war) that had not been institutionalized. To make matters worse, the policy makers were often thoughtless, ill informed and given to making snap judgments. On the other hand, the professional administrators often failed to provide necessary information and thwarted the timely implementation of decisions by hiding behind the impregnable walls of bureaucratic routine.

The shortcomings of the bureaucracy were due in part to the fact that in origin and in mentality it was a bureaucracy of estate managers. The first professional, or semiprofessional, officials were those who collected revenues from the domain. The administration of justice, the keeping of the peace, local defense — all were thought of as being part of the work of preserving and drawing a maximum revenue from the domain. The sheriff in England, the *prévôt* in France appear a long time before professional judges, and an even longer time before permanent military and police officials. The first requirement of the rulers who laid the foundations of the medieval state was to secure regular and adequate revenues. It was only when such revenues were available that larger and stronger political units could be built, and good estate management was therefore the foundation for all other institutions.

The estate manager mentality was thus essential in the early stages of state-building, but it was a mentality with dangerous limitations. It loved routine and stability; it resented fluctuation and flexibility. The ideal situation for the estate manager was one in which a register could be prepared listing all sources of income so that this fixed income could be collected year after year. Once the great effort had been made to prepare a list or lists of sources of income there was reluctance to make new lists. The old ones were patched up and corrected, but they were never really brought up to date. This meant that theoretical totals of revenues in the rolls were meaningless because over the years lands or rights had been acquired, or more often, given away.

On the whole, however, such attitudes did little harm as long as income came primarily from the domain. Land, a local court, a town marketplace — such things did not vanish even if officials were working with records that went back a century or two. Changes in the domain were gradual enough so that they could be remembered even if the basic records were not revised. In a period in which prices were rising only slowly a fixed income based on conventional valuations was not a disaster; it was better than the decline in income which would have occurred if the estate managers had not done their work conscientiously.

The situation became very different when rulers began to depend on taxation. Now what was needed was a new estimate (of hearths, lands, income, and the like) every time there was a new tax. Great variations in income were to be expected, especially if experiments were tried with different kinds of taxes. The old bureaucracy could not adjust to the new demands made upon it. Granted, there was serious understaffing; granted, also, that the propertied classes tried to dodge taxes by various devices. Nevertheless, after a promising start, the tendency to use conventional estimates and to accept conventional sums offered by local authorities became dominant. By the middle of the fourteenth century the number of hearths listed in France or the amount of personal property assessed in England bore no relationship to the real facts.[10] The yield of ordinary taxes decreased, and even in time of peace, governments were chronically short of money. In periods of emergency, when large sums were required, no one had any idea of what the resources of the country were, or how they could be tapped.

The estate manager mentality was reinforced by respect for custom and precedent. This respect was strong in all elements of society, and it received legal status through the work of the courts of law. After an early period of innovation and experiment the courts became reasonably satisfied with their jurisprudence and procedures, and grew resistant to change. Moreover, in both France and England the growth of the power of royal courts had been aided by their protection of *seisin*, that is, well-established possession, or, to define it even more broadly, protection of the existing order of things. This rule of law helped to make the courts popular with the propertied classes, since customary rights, regional, local, and personal privileges all came under the formula. Preservation of local customs and special privileges was often inconvenient, but this was the price that European rulers paid for their use of law as a means of state-building. As long as powerful subjects resisted the law, the law could be used to break them, but when the propertied classes turned to the law to protect their powers and privileges, the government often found itself thwarted or delayed in carrying out its policies.[11] Once again we find lack of flexibility and resistance to change supported by an important element in the bureaucracy.

Moreover, like almost every other medieval group with special skills and knowledge, the bureaucrats developed something very like a guild system. Each branch of the government tended to become a closed association, with members recruited largely from the families, friends and protégés of men already in office. Every department tried to secure special privileges which removed it from the direct control of the policy makers and protected the tenure of office of its members. The ruler could, of course, always promote lesser officials to higher places or remove men from key offices. But corporate spirit was so strong that these changes often had little effect; the new head of the office was bound to follow long-established precedents.

Finally, it was difficult to secure adequate cooperation between central and local officials. Local officials were often burdened with too many duties and they often identified themselves with local interests. This was especially true in England, where sheriffs, tax collectors, and justices of the peace were unpaid local notables. But even in France, where the local bureaucracy was composed (at least in theory) of men drawn from outside the province in which they served, men who made a reasonable profit out of their offices and who could hope for promotion to Paris, we find the same tendency to favor local interests. Many orders from the center were not obeyed, or were obeyed only after long delays. Many requests for information were never answered. Probably the greatest inefficiencies in late medieval government were to be found at the local level.[12]

We can see, then, that the bureaucrats often failed to acquire up-to-date information, that they were inclined to lean heavily on old precedents, and that they were apt to be more interested in preserving their privileges than in administrative reform. The policy makers, on the other hand, were not very well equipped to make reforms in government, or indeed to make policy of any kind. Policy was made by the ruler and his Council, and well into the fifteenth century Council members were erratic in their attendance as well as in their decisions. The heads of established departments of government were regular members of Councils, but seldom had a decisive voice in policy making. The bureaucrats were there to give information — a task which they often performed badly — and to discuss the ways and means of implementing decisions taken by others. The great (and expensive) problems of peace and war, truces and alliances, were determined by the king and the leading members of the aristocracy — princes of the blood, heads of baronial factions, royal favorites. Such men were not inclined to work very hard at acquiring information or to be very diligent in seeing that their directives were obeyed. They were, on the other hand, eager to get their share of royal gifts, pensions, and high military commands. The irresponsibility of the policy makers reached its height when the king was weak or incapable, for example, in the reigns of Charles VI of France or Henry VI of England.[13] But even strong and able kings who had chosen the best councillors they could find did not make very wise policy decisions during much of the fourteenth and fifteenth centuries. They did not reform their administrative or financial systems, they did not develop new organs of government which were badly needed (e.g., for military operations), and their foreign policy was often disastrous.

It is only fair to add that both policy makers and bureaucrats were operating in a very difficult economic climate. From about 1300 to about 1450 there was a great depression in western Europe. There were, of course, fluctuations. Some towns or regions were relatively prosperous while others were in misery; some periods of modest recovery were interlarded between periods of utter poverty. But, by and large, all European governments experienced years of acute financial distress in the fourteenth and fifteenth centuries and this distress did not encourage reform or innovation. If reform meant delay —

as it usually did — it had to be rejected. It was better to get fifty thousand pounds at once by sloppy methods, such as tax farming, than to get one hundred thousand pounds two years later by instituting better methods of assessment and collection. Any innovation that involved a continuing expense was likewise impossible to adopt. Certainly the advantages of a standing army were realized by the fourteenth century, but no medieval state could be sure that it would have enough money to pay its soldiers every year. (Indeed, most early modern states found it difficult to pay members of their armed forces with any regularity). It is thus not entirely a paradox to say that states of the fourteenth and early fifteenth centuries could not afford to be efficient. And it is obvious that the economic revival that began in the latter part of the fifteenth century made it easier to remedy some of the deficiencies of the earlier period.

One should not, however, exaggerate either the weaknesses of late medieval states or the virtues of the states of the early modern period. The medieval state, with all its faults, had been strong enough to survive and the early modern state inherited both the strength and the faults. The more one looks at the "New Monarchies" the less newness is visible. Most of the work of government continued to be performed much as it had before; administrative structures were changed very slowly when they were changed at all. No sixteenth-century state was very well organized; no sixteenth-century government was very efficient.

Yet it is undeniable that in the sixteenth century, European states gained power, took on new responsibilities, and received increased respect from their subjects. These successes were due far less to administrative reforms than to changes in the attitudes and behavior of both the governing group and those who were governed.

The policy making body — the Council — had been, as we have said, both erratic and irresponsible. But the very volatility of the Council meant that it could easily be remodeled. The Council had none of the rigidity of a Court of King's Bench or a *Parlement*; its composition and its powers varied according to the wishes of the king and the balance of political factions. Thus when the "New Monarchs" tried to increase their power and authority, the first and obvious step was to make the Council a more effective organ of government. If there was anything new in the "New Monarchies," it was the new personnel of the Council, men who worked at their jobs and knew how to do their work. The old bureaus and bureaucrats continued to perform their old functions, but a new bureaucracy began to emerge from the Council — a bureaucracy that was more amenable to the wishes of the ruler and better prepared to cope with the problems of the early modern world.

The change was gradual, and at times imperceptible. For ceremonial occasions the Council looked much as it always had, only more so; it included all the great officers of state and large numbers of the higher nobility. But the working Council or Councils (duties were often divided among two or more groups) became more and more professionalized. Policy was made by the king and a relatively small number of men who realized that to be a Councillor was a full-time job. The fringe members of the Council — those who appeared only occasionally — either had little influence or were used as expert advisers in areas where they had special knowledge.

The most professional, and often the most powerful, members of the new type of Council were the Secretaries of State.[14] Originally personal servants of the king, they had retained a close relationship with the monarch and a thorough knowledge of the affairs of state while gaining prestige and authority. The essential elements of the new bureaucracy may be discerned most easily in the offices and the entourage of the Secretaries; most of the new departments of government grew out of their activity.

The Secretaries' prime duty was to preserve the security of the state against internal and external enemies. They had very little to work with in the way of armed forces. Standing armies were small and scattered; England had none at all. No country had an adequate police force, and local militias or levies of country gentlemen were effective only against groups as ill trained and poorly organized as they were. Order was preserved less by the use of force than by the acquisition of timely knowledge and the establishment of a network of personal relationships between the Secretaries (and other working members of the Council) and local authorities.

The effort to obtain exact and early information was one of the most striking changes in the attitudes of policy makers. We are all aware of the methods that were used — permanent ambassadors, secret agents both at home and abroad, constant correspondence with knowledgeable people — but we may forget that much of the expense was borne by individual members of the Council rather than by the government. Even the Secretaries did not have adequate staffs, and other members of the Council had even less support. But political power went to the well-informed and ambitious men who were willing to spend some of their own money to be well informed. A certain part of the new bureaucracy was thus composed of protégés and personal clerks of the policy makers — a tradition that lasted in diplomatic missions almost to our own day.

Armed with precise information, supported by clients in every part of the country, the Secretaries and other Councillors could secure considerably more uniformity in the execution of policy than had been possible earlier. They could also begin to control overmighty subjects and suppress the disorders and plotting that had led to rebellion in psat centuries. In performing these functions most Councils found it desirable to draw on the residual judicial power still vested in the sovereign and to act as courts of summary justice. Internal security was not the only reason for developing these new jurisdictions; the unfathomable technicalities and the interminable delays of courts of customary law had created a demand for speedier and cheaper justice. But the preservation of internal security was the factor that made the conciliar courts both necessary and popular.[15]

This point brings us to the other aspect of state-building in the sixteenth century — a somewhat changed concept of sovereignty and of the functions of the state. The shift was subtle, gradual, and much less clear-cut than some historians of political theory have claimed. The right to give final judgment in lawsuits was still important, as Henry VIII emphasized in his attack on the papacy.[16] The right to make law was perhaps more important than it had been earlier, but, in spite of the admirers of Bodin, I do not think that this was the essential element in sixteenth-century ideas of sovereignty.

The real change was a great increase in the willingness of the governed to accept arbitrary acts of executive power. Even this was not a complete innovation; as Jolliffe has shown, arbitrary exercise of executive power was common in England in the twelfth century.[17] But it is significant that while in the fourteenth century the "prerogative" referred largely to the king's right to control the administration and the appointment of high officials, in the sixteenth and seventeenth centuries, it referred to his right to take extraordinary steps to defend the state.[18] This was not entirely a new concept; as Gaines Post has shown, "reason of state" was accepted as an adequate excuse for arbitrary actions in the thirteenth century.[19] But thirteenth-century rulers used their extraordinary powers only within very narrow limits; not until the sixteenth century could "reason of state" be used to justify interference with the religious beliefs or the economic activity of the subject. And, curiously enough, this interference was accepted as right and proper even by those who suffered from it. Most of the men executed for opposing the sovereign went to their deaths affirming their loyalty to him.[20]

It was this increase in executive authority that kept the Council, or at least the chief members of the Council, so busy that a new bureaucracy had to be created. It was simply impossible to deal with all the problems of foreign affairs, permanent armies and navies, internal security, and economic controls without hiring men who could not be fitted in to the old-line departments. Obviously, there was bound to be friction between the old and the new bureaucrats. The new bureaucrats threatened the independence and lessened the prestige of the old bureaucrats.

The new bureaucrats had no respect for the solemn procedures and traditional privileges that protected the corporate identity of the older departments of government. The new bureaucrats were perhaps more intelligent and probably better educated than the old bureaucrats. Certainly they were more likely to have had the new education of the Renaissance than the old education of the Middle Ages; they were more likely to speak the new language of unlimited prerogative powers than the old language of sovereignty limited by law.

One point needs to be stressed because it was especially irritating — the lack of specialization in the new bureaucracy. Again, the Secretaries of State offer a good example of the problem. Since security was indivisible they had responsibilities for both internal and external affairs and hence could intervene in any area of government — finance, justice, local administration, diplomacy, and war. Thus the formation of departments dealing specifically with external relations or with defense was delayed — one Secretary might be in charge of negotiations with one group of countries while another Secretary dealt with another foreign area.[21] King and Council were supposed to coordinate the work of the Secretaries and to make final policy decisions, but the process of coordination could be slow and difficult. Few men, however, were bothered by delay in organizing a Foreign Office or a War Office, while many were irritated by the fact that the Council as a whole and the Secretaries in particular had roving commissions. They could intervene in any situation where they thought the welfare of the state was concerned. The unpredictability of intervention was as annoying as the fact of intervention. A department whose normal processes were interrupted intermittently was more apt to make trouble than a department which had had to surrender some of its functions permanently. When, in the seventeenth and eighteenth centuries, the new bureaucracy became organized into departments with specific missions operating under regular procedures, friction between old and new bureaucrats disappeared.

Until that time, however, there was competition and at times an open struggle between the two groups. Neither the council-centered bureaucracy nor the old corporative bureaucracy could expect to displace its rival completely. The Council and its offshoots could not attend to all the details that were handled by the old departments of finance and justice. The old departments could not coordinate and direct policy as could the Council. There had to be a division of functions, and the nature of the division affected the future structure of most European states. The more that was done by the Council and by departments derived from the Council, the more powerful was the sovereign, and, on the whole, the more efficient was the administration of the state. The more the power of the Council, especially in judicial matters, was curtailed, the easier it was to limit the power of the ruler, though at the cost of some inefficiency. The political crises of the seventeenth century in England and in France were in part (and only in part) caused by competition between the old and the new bureaucracies. The different outcome of those crises was registered in the absolute monarchy of Louis XIV and the limited monarchy of William and Mary.

BY JOSEPH R. STRAYER

NOTES

1. Most early Christian writers accepted Cicero's statement that a commonwealth is created "juris consensu" ("by acceptance of law"). Even Augustine, who doubted that justice could exist among pagans, said once that without justice a kingdom was simply large-scale robbery ("Remota itaque justitia quid sunt regna nisi magna latrocinia?"). Isidore of Seville, who was quoted much more often than Augustine on this point, used Cicero's definition, and added that the object of government is to do justice. On these writers see R. W. and A. J. Carlyle, *History of Medieval Political Theory in the West* (Edinburgh and London, 1930), Chs. 1, 14, 18, and C. H. McIlwain, *Growth of Political Thought in the West* (New York, 1932), pp. 114-18, 154-60, 173-74.

2. These ideas, common to almost all medieval thinkers, were stated most clearly by Thomas Aquinas in the *Summa Theologica,* I-II, questions 90-97. In the translation by A. C. Pegis, *Basic Writings of Saint Thomas Aquinas,* 2 vols. (New York, 1945), the essential propositions may be found in II, 742-52. See esp. 748, "the government of things in God, the ruler of the universe, has the nature of a law"; 750, "this participation of the eternal law in the rational creature is called the natural law"; 751, "from the precepts of the natural law . . . the human reason needs to proceed to the more particular determination of certain matters. These particular determinations . . . are called human laws."

3. The classic example is Magna Carta; thus in 1297, when Edward I had used somewhat inadequate procedures for obtaining consent to a tax, the magnates resisted, asked for confirmation of Magna Carta, and in the confirmation secured the acknowledgment that aids could be taken only "par commun assent de tout le roiaume" (Stubbs, *Select Charters,* 9th ed. [Oxford, 1921], pp. 490-93).

4. For example, the Statute of *Quia Emptores,* 1290, changed the whole law of real property in England by forbidding subinfeudation (text in Stubbs, *Select Charters,* p. 473, a very useful discussion in T. F. T. Plucknett, *Legislation of Edward I* [Oxford, 1949], pp. 102-08). In France the complicated problem of alienation of noble land to churchmen and commoners was settled by a series of royal ordinances that not only increased the profits of the crown by charging fees for such alienations but also gave royal officials an excuse to intervene in every part of the realm. The first two laws of 1275 and 1291 are printed in *Ordonnances des Rois de France* (Paris, 1723ff.), I, 303, 323. There were many later acts. For a discussion of the problem see Brussel, *Nouvel examen de l'usage général des fiefs,* (Paris, 1727), I, 657-74.

5. *Les Olim,* ed. A. Beugnot (Paris, 1839-48), II, 5-6; one of Philip's grievances that led him to seize Aquitaine in 1294 was the attempt by agents of the king of England to prevent appeals to the court of France, Beugnot, 28ff.; an appeal by the burgesses of Ghent to the king of France in 1296 gave Philip a chance to put pressure on the court of Flanders and eventually led to the (temporary) seizure of the county. See also P. Chaplais, "La souveraineté du roi de France et le

pouvoir legislatif en Guyenne au début du XIVᵉ siecle," *Le Moyen Age,* LXIX (1963), 449-467.

6. See M. Powicke, *The Thirteenth Century* (Oxford, 1953), pp. 608-16, and the cases cited there.

7. For a discussion of this subject see J. R. Strayer, "Laicization of French and English Society in the Thirteenth Century," *Speculum* XV (1940), 76-86.

8. P. Dupuy, *Histoire du differend d'entre le pape Boniface VIII et Philippes le Bel* (Paris, 1655), pp. 309, 310, 312. Guillaume de Nogaret, writing shortly after 1305, said repeatedly that everyone is bound to defend his fatherland ("quisque teneatur patriam suam defendere"), Archives Nationales, Paris, J350, no. 10; at about the same time the king said even the clergy owed material aid for defense of the kingdom.

9. *Registres du pape Boniface VIII,* no. 2354, bull *Etsi de statu,* 31 July 1297, allowed the king in case of necessity to tax the clergy for defense of the realm. The king (or his Council if he were a minor) could determine when such an emergency occurred. Thomas Aquinas had reached this conclusion a generation earlier; in the *De regimine Judaeorum* (ed. in A. Passerin d'Entrèves, *San Tommaso d'Aquino, Scritti Politici* [Bologna, 1946], p. 47) he says a ruler can levy special taxes for the common welfare or for defense.

10. For conventional valuation in England see J. F. Willard, *Parliamentary Taxes on Personal Property* (Cambridge, 1934), pp. 5-6, 138-41. On the artificial nature of the *feux* (hearths) in France, see the remarks of A. Vuitry, *Etudes sur le régime financier de la France* II, (Paris, 1883), 167-70.

11. On this problem, see my study on *Les gens de justice du Languedoc* (Toulouse, 1970). A good example was the lawsuit over royal rights in the county of Gévaudan, which began in 1269, was supposedly ended by a compromise in 1307, was revived by an appeal of the nobles of the county, and was finally settled in 1341; see R. Michel, *L'administration royale dans la sénéchaussée de Beaucaire* (Paris, 1910), pp. 175-81, 454-58, and J. Roucaute, *Lettres de Philippe le Bel relatives au pays de Gévaudan* (Mende, 1897), pp. viii-x.

12. As J. R. Major pointed out in *Representative Institutions in Renaissance France 1421-1559* (Madison, Wisc., 1960), pp. 7-13.

13. Maurice Rey, *Les finances royales sous Charles VI: Les causes du déficit* (Paris, 1965), esp. pp. 571-607. See also the books by Françoise Lehoux (*Jean de France, duc de Berri* [Paris, 1966]) and Richard Vaughan (*Philip the Bold* [Cambridge, Mass., 1962], *John the Fearless* [New York, 1966]).

14. For the secretaries in England, see F. M. G. Evans, *The Principal Secretary of State 1558-1680* (Manchester, 1923), and the remarkable studies of Conyers Read, *Mr. Secretary Cecil and Queen Elizabeth* (New York, 1955), and *Mr. Secretary Walsingham,* 3 vols. (Oxford, 1925). A contemporary description of the duties of the secretary may be found in I, 423-43. For the secretaries in France, the old work of Fauvelet du Toc, *Histoire des Secrétaires d'Estat* (Paris, 1668), is still useful. See also H. de Lucay, *Des origines du pouvoir ministériel en France: Les Secré-*

taires d'Etat depuis leur institution jusqu'à la mort de Louis XV (Paris, 1881). For individual careers, J. Nouaillac, *Villeroy, secrétaire d'Etat et ministre de Charles IX, Henri III et Henri IV* (Paris, 1909), and G. Robertet, *Les Robertets au XVIe siècle* (Paris, 1888).

15. In England, for example, the Court of Star Chamber was popular throughout the sixteenth century; see W. Holdsworth, *A History of English Law*, V (London, 1937), 155-214, and esp. 189-90.

16. The Act in Restraint of Appeals, 1553, is one of the strongest assertions of sovereignty in the Tudor period, but it is based on the king's right "to render and to yield justice and final determination to all manner of folk residents or subjects within this his realm. . . ." (*Statutes of the Realm* [London, 1810-28], III, 427).

17. J. E. A. Jolliffe, *Angevin Kingship*, 2nd ed. (London, 1963), esp. ch. 3 ("Vis et Voluntas") and ch. 4 ("Ira et Malevolentia").

18. C. Stephenson and F. G. Marcham, *Sources of English Constitutional History* (New York, 1937), pp. 216-17, 238-39; both Edward III in 1343 and Richard II in 1386 asserted that limitations on the king's right to appoint his officials were contrary to his prerogative; *Stephenson and Marcham*, pp. 424, 426, 436, arguments over the king's prerogative right to tax imports at will. See esp. p. 436 (opinion of Chief Baron Fleming): "The king's power is double, ordinary and absolute. . . . The absolute power is that which is applied to the general benefit of the people. . . . And this power is most properly named policy and government."

19. Gaines Post, *Studies in Medieval Political Thought* (Princeton, N.J., 1964), pp. 241-309, esp. pp. 303-7.

20. Lacey Baldwin Smith, "English Treason Trials and Confessions in the Sixteenth Century," *Journal of the History of Ideas*, XV (1954), 471-98.

21. Thus the French during part of the sixteenth century had four secretaries, each charged with security in one section of the kingdom and with relations with the states bordering on his section. Later the English had a Secretary for the Northern Department (north Europe) and a Secretary for the Southern Department (not only south Europe but also the American Colonies). There was no Foreign Office in England until 1782. The French had a permanent Foreign Office as early as 1626.

BIBLIOGRAPHY

Allen, J. W. *A History of Political Thought in the Sixteenth Century*. London, 1928.

Carlyle, A. J., and R. W. *A History of Mediaeval Political Theory in the West*. 6 vols. Edinburgh and London, 1903-36.

Cazelles, R. *La société politique et la crise de la royauté sous Philipe de Valois*. Paris, 1958.

Chrimes, S. B. *English Constitutional Ideas in the Fifteenth Century*. Cambridge, 1936.

Chrimes, S. B. *An Introduction to the Administrative History of Mediaeval England.* Oxford, 1952.

Church, W. F. *Constitutional Thought in Sixteenth-Century France.* Cambridge, Mass., 1941.

David, M. *La Souveraineté et les limites juridiques du pouvoir monarchique du IXe au XVe siècle.* Paris, 1954.

Declareuil, J. *Histoire générale du droit français des origines à 1789.* Paris, 1925.

Doucet, R. *Les Institutions de la France au XVIe siècle.* 2 vols. Paris, 1925.

Elton, G. R. *The Tudor Constitution.* Cambridge, 1960.

———. *The Tudor Revolution in Government.* Cambridge, 1953.

Kantorowicz, E. H. *The King's Two Bodies: A Study in Medieval Political Theology.* Princeton, N.J., 1957.

Lot, F., and R. Fawtier. *Histoire des institutions françaises au moyen âge,* II: *Institutions royales.* Paris, 1958.

Olivier-Martin, F. *Histoire du droit français des origines à la Révolution.* Paris, 1948.

Petit-Dutaillis, C. *The Feudal Monarchy in France and England.* London, 1936.

Post, G. *Studies in Medieval Legal Thought.* Princeton, N.J., 1964.

Rey, M. *Les finances royales sous Charles VI: les causes du déficit, 1388-1413.* Paris, 1965.

Strayer, J. R. "Defense of the realm and royal power in France," in *Studi in Onore di Gino Luzzatto,* I (Milan, 1950), 289-97.

———. "The Historical Experience of Nation-Building in Europe," in *Nation-Building,* ed. K. W. Deutsch and W. J. Foltz (New York, 1963), pp. 17-26.

Tout, T. F. *Chapters in the Administrative History of Mediaeval England.* 6 vols. Manchester, 1920-1933.

Valois, N. *Le conseil du Roi au XIVe, XVe, et XVIe siècle.* Paris, 1888.

Wilks, M. *The Problem of Sovereignty in the Later Middle Ages.* Cambridge, 1963.

The Impact of Early Italian Humanism on Thought and Learning

or some time the so-called problem of the Renaissance, and the meaning of Renaissance humanism, have been the subject of much debate and controversy, as I do not have to remind you. I shall do my best in this paper to keep away from these controversial questions, but I am afraid I shall not be able to avoid them altogether. Hence I must ask you to forgive me if I repeat some of the points I have made in writing or in speaking on other occasions.[1] On the so-called problem of the Renaissance, I shall say nothing, except for calling your attention to a recent paper by François Masai who attempts to distinguish between the Renaissance as a period and the Renaissance as a movement, a distinction that helps to resolve certain difficulties and surely deserves careful study.[2] As to Renaissance humanism, I shall, as always, refuse to take it as the forerunner of all the nice and ill-defined ideas that nowadays go by that name, but rather interpret it as the intellectual movement that during the Renaissance was associated with the rise and expansion of the hu-

manities, the *studia humanitatis*, a well-defined cycle of scholarly disciplines. Renaissance humanism was basically a cultural, literary, and scholarly movement. It overlapped with philosophy, and had an impact on it, but it should not be identified with philosophy. I cannot agree with those scholars who treat humanism exclusively or primarily as a period in the history of philosophy, nor with those who tend to deny that humanism had any role or significance in the history of philosophy.[3] There are many Renaissance philosophers who were to a greater or smaller extent affected by humanism, to be sure, but whose work and thought essentially fall outside the framework of humanism, and this description applies not only to the Aristotelians, but also to the Platonists such as Cusanus, Ficino, or Pico, and to the philosophers of nature such as Telesio or Bruno. Vice versa, it would be wrong to deny that some humanists, such as Petrarch, Salutati, or Bruni, Valla, or Alberti, made significant contributions to philosophical thought. Yet in talking about the humanists, we should never forget that even the work of those humanists who contributed most to philosophy comprised many subjects that are outside the area of philosophy, at least by Greek, medieval, or contemporary standards, and that besides these humanist thinkers, if I may be allowed to use this term, there was a very large number, perhaps a majority, of genuine humanists, who made important contributions to literature or learning, but few or none to philosophy.[4] I cannot help taking this view of humanism again as my starting point, although I know that it has been widely criticized. I think it is based on rather broad evidence, that is, on the literary production of the humanists, on the records of their professional activities, and on the content of their teaching and of their libraries. I am quite ready to modify my views if I am confronted with valid evidence of a similar nature, but I venture to remain unimpressed when I am told by eminent colleagues that they find my views distasteful or prosaic, or if younger colleagues or students try to quibble about definitions without knowing or even suspecting the large body of textual, bibliographical, and documentary evidence which these definitions are trying to approximate, if not to accommodate.

I am afraid even if our conference succeeds in avoiding a general debate on the Renaissance and on humanism, it may very well become involved, and perhaps bogged down in, a new controversy about the early Renaissance and early humanism, as compared with their later phases. I suspect the content and time limits of the early Renaissance and of early humanism might be as hard to define or to agree upon as those of the larger period or movement itself. I confess that unlike some of my colleagues in history, I am not deeply disturbed by problems of periodization, but it is obviously important that we state as clearly as possible what the subject of our discussion is going to be. Some historians begin the Renaissance with the sixteenth century, others with the fifteenth, and again others go even further back, and their notion of the early Renaissance will vary accordingly. In a similar way, we may have early humanism begin with Bruni, or with Salutati, or with Petrarch, or with the so-called prehumanists such as Lovato and Mussato. Depending on these views, the fifteenth century, which by all standards is the high point of Renaissance humanism, may appear to be either late or intermediary or early. I prefer to use the most inclusive definition of humanism, extending it from about 1280 to 1600, and hence treat the period from 1280 to 1500 as that of early humanism. I shall not consider the humanism of the sixteenth century as early, but shall occasionally make references to it since it was the continuation of early humanism and sometimes helps to illustrate the impact of the latter. This broader chronological framework also helps us to understand the impact of Italian humanism outside of Italy. There may be a debate about the role of Italy within the Renaissance as a whole, but there can be no question about the primacy of Italy in Renaissance humanism. Now some traces of the influence of Italian humanism outside of Italy have been identified even during the fourteenth century, especially in Bohemia and in France,[5] but there seems to be wide agreement that the full impact of Italian humanism in the rest of Western Europe was felt only after the middle of the fifteenth and during the sixteenth centuries.

Before discussing my topic, I should like to remind the reader of the subjects with which the humanists were professionally concerned, and of the place these subjects occupied on the intellectual globe of the Middle Ages and of the Renaissance. The modern term "humanism" as applied to the Renaissance is derived from the term "humanist" that was coined in the late fifteenth century, and the term "humanist" was derived in turn from the term *studia humanitatis* that survives in a somewhat diluted fashion in our humanities.[6] The term *studia humanitatis* is of ancient Roman origin, and it was revived and given a more specific meaning in the early fifteenth century.[7]

The cycle of the humanities (grammar, rhetoric, poetry, history, and moral philosophy) can be explicitly documented from the fifteenth century on, but there are less explicit testimonies that prove, for example, that Petrarch, in the eyes of his contemporaries, was active in these very same fields.[8] The often heard remark that the *studia humanitatis* of the Renaissance are but another name for the seven liberal arts of the Middle Ages is but partly true. For the *studia humanitatis* omit not only the mathematical disciplines of the quadrivium, but also logic or dialectic, and they add three subjects that are at best implied in the trivium, namely, poetry, history, and moral philosophy. Moreover, it was only in the early Middle Ages that the seven liberal arts were considered as the sum total of secular learning, whereas in the high Middle Ages, after the rise of the universities, new subjects were added to the list: law, medicine, theology, and the various philosophical disciplines, especially natural philosophy, metaphysics, and ethics. For a movement arising in a period that, depending on our preference or perspective, may be called the late Middle Ages or the Early Renaissance, the fact that it omits from the center of its attention five of the seven liberal arts is probably less significant than that it also omits all of the newer university disciplines except ethics. Now I have never said, as some critics believe, that the humanists restricted their activity to the subjects called the humanities, let alone that the humanistic movement had no impact apart from these subjects. Yet I have found it necessary, for the sake of clarity, to distinguish between the achievement of the humanists within their own professional area, the humanities, and their influence on other fields outside of that area. For this same reason, I shall also try to survey my subject along three different lines, and speak first of the achievement of Italian humanism within its own domain, the humanities; second, of the diffusion of Italian humanism outside of Italy; and finally, of the impact of humanism, both in Italy and in other countries, on other fields of learning, and especially on theology, philosophy, and the sciences.

Italian humanism, according to the view I am trying to propose, began towards the end of the thirteenth century with the so-called prehumanists of Padua, Verona, and other neighboring cities. This first period, which extended roughly to the middle of the fourteenth century, includes the work of such scholars as Albertino Mussato at Padua and Giovanni del Virgilio at Bologna,[9] and I venture to add that Dante, in several aspects of his work, seems to be affected by this earliest phase of humanism.[10] The second phase comprises the later fourteenth century, beginning with Petrarch and including Boccaccio, Salutati, and many lesser figures. The third phase is the humanism of the early fifteenth century, with Bruni, Marsuppini, and Poggio; Barzizza and Guarino; Valla and Filelfo; Enea Silvio; Alberti and Manetti. Finally, the humanism of the later fifteenth century is represented, not by its metaphysicians such as Ficino or Pico, but by its scholars, poets, and moralists such as Pontano and Poliziano; Landino, Scala and Fonzio; Ermolao Barbaro, Battista Mantovano, Giorgio Merula, and numerous others whose names are less well known.

It is admittedly not easy to bring the vast and diversified activities of these scholars and their lesser contemporaries under a single denominator, but I am convinced that we must try to keep all their achievements in mind when we want to generalize, and must not merely overemphasize some features that have a special appeal for us, at the same time omitting others that may be less appealing or fashionable.

When we look at early Italian humanism as a whole, a number of aspects emerge that are characteristic of the movement and of the entire period, although it would be wrong to claim that there were no medieval precedents for them. What seems most obvious to me is a shift in the balance of interest and in the emphasis given to a group of studies, the humanities, that came to occupy a central place in education, in literature, and to some extent in professional life, and that represented a peculiar combination of interests that does not have a single counterpart either in the Middle Ages or in modern times. Humanism combines in its aspirations and in its achievements literary skill, historical and philological scholarship, and moral wisdom: three pursuits that for us are quite distinct, but that for the humanists were inseparable. Literary skill was to some extent teachable, and it was of tremendous concern to the humanists, for it served for the effective expression, in speech and in writing, in verse and in prose, in Latin and in the vernacular languages, of any chosen content of ideas and images, of feelings, or of events. Wisdom must be combined with eloquence, as many humanists kept repeating, and as Ermolao Barbaro argued against Pico.[11] We are accustomed to the idea that literary style is unimportant for the philosopher or scientist or theologian, as compared with the validity of his ideas; we could cite many ancient, medieval, and modern authorities in support of our view, and we may even be right. It is a view that may help us to understand medieval scholastic philosophy (and Pico would be on our side), but it will completely prevent us from properly understanding Italian humanism and its contribution to philosophical or general thought. Moreover, according to the humanists, eloquence and wisdom were inextricably linked with classical scholarship, with history and philology, for the humanists were deeply convinced that both wisdom and eloquence, the content and the form of writing, depended on the study and imitation of the ancient Greek and Latin authors. Vice versa, the deep concern for the attainment of wisdom and eloquence, along with the conviction that both can best be learned from the ancients, gave to classical scholarship a degree of "relevance" that it has hardly had either before or afterwards. I am inclined to go even one step further: the thought of the humanists is inseparable from their literary and scholarly concerns, just as the thought of the scholastic philosophers is inseparable from their theology, or that of the seventeenth-century philosophers from their physics. Renaissance thought, at least in its humanist sector, is a handmaiden of the humanities, not of theology as some medieval philosophy, nor of the sciences as much of modern philosophy.

When we speak of the humanist contribution to learning we must include, and begin with, their modest but vast work as copyists, printers, and editors, and the reform of handwriting which they brought about.[12] The fact that we read and write Roman and Italic rather than Gothic characters is due to the humanists and probably represents their most lasting and pervasive, though least recognized, contribution to modern Western civilization.

I shall merely mention the vast amount of straight literary compositions left to us by the humanists, and emphasize the fact that many humanists, some of them quite famous, left nothing else but this: letters and speeches, plays and dialogues, epical, didactic, and lyrical poems as well as epigrams. Their numerous works of history and biography served a scholarly as well as a literary purpose.[13] They tried to examine the evidence and to ascertain the true facts, and Valla's treatise on the donation of Constantine may serve as a famous example of their contribution to critical scholarship in history. They wrote on Latin and Greek grammar, on rhetoric and mythology, and on other topics related to classical antiquity, but even more important is their work on the actual text of the Latin and Greek classical writers.[14] They rediscovered a number of ancient Latin texts, some of them important, such as Lucretius or Tacitus, and they practically acquired for the West the knowledge of the Greek language and of classical Greek literature.[15] They gave to the classical texts a wide diffusion in manuscript and in print. They collated and evaluated the older manuscripts of the classical authors and developed great skill in emending their texts, thus laying the ground for the modern methods of textual criticism.[16] In lecturing about the ancient texts, they produced a vast body of commentaries that have not yet been studied for their method or their relation to earlier or later works of a comparable nature. They also translated into Latin practically the entire extant body of Greek classical literature, introducing the Greek poets, orators, and historians into the mainstream of Western scholarship and education.[17] I cannot here repeat what Voigt, Sabbadini, Ullman, and others have written about this subject, but I am convinced that the contribution of the Italian humanists to classical scholarship, and the importance of this contribution within the total achievement of the humanists, has been greatly underestimated by most modern historians including even Jacob Burckhardt. When we read what some historians of political or philosophical thought tell us about Bruni or Valla, we are apt to forget that Bruni wrote many letters, some orations, and even a few poems, and translated Plutarch and Demosthenes, in addition to Plato and Aristotle;[18] or that Valla wrote the *Elegantiae*, his most popular work down to the eighteenth century, and translated Herodotus and Thucydides.

Yet let us pass from literature and learning to the domain of thought. The humanists considered moral philosophy as a province of their domain, and that included social and political thought as well as some problems of education and of religion. We have important writings on these subjects by Petrarch and Salutati, by Bruni and Poggio, by Valla and Manetti, by Alberti, Pontano, and many others. I agree with those scholars who have emphasized the large number of interesting ideas found in these treatises,[19] and the extent to which they differ in content and in form from medieval literature. I also agree that it is significant that some problems traditionally reserved for religious literature were now discussed in a strictly secular context, and that certain problems and topics came to the foreground that reflect the peculiar concerns and attitudes of the humanists and of their contemporaries: reason and fortune, the dignity and misery of man, the relative merits of republic and monarchy, of nobility and personal merit, of the

active and contemplative life, of different human values
and professions. I also recognize a common style and ideal
in the emphasis on classical models and quotations, and
on personal feeling and experience (this is, I think, the
meaning of the individualism which Burckhardt found
in the Renaissance and which has been so much debated
by his critics; I find it prominent in Petrarch and even in
Dante). Yet I cannot agree when it is suggested that
Italian humanism may be characterized by a uniform set
of specific ideas that would make it appear as a kind of
secular or even antireligious ideology, consistently opposed to medieval values, and a harbinger of the enlightenment, of nineteenth-century liberalism, or what the
twentieth century likes rather than understands under the
name of humanism. Salutati and Bruni, to be sure, defend
Florence and her republican liberty, and it is important
that Renaissance humanism includes these voices.[20] Yet
we should not forget that Loschi and Decembrio, less
famous but no less humanistic, defended Milan and her
monarchic rulers. Poggio praised Scipio, but Guarino
answered with a praise of Caesar. Poggio, Landino, and
others praised personal merit against nobility, but Lauro
Querini defended nobility in its Venetian form,[21]
Tristano Caracciolo in its Neapolitan form,[22] and the
best known of all treatises by Buonaccorso da Montemagno (it was even translated into English and other
languages in the fifteenth century) left the question undecided.[23] What is common to all humanists is not so
much a set of specific opinions, but rather a common
style and taste, a common set of problems, and a common
set of ancient sources from which everybody felt free to
borrow. The best we may say is that of two alternatives

among which most medieval authors would have rejected one, also the latter now began to find its defenders. I may be allowed to add an embarrassing detail that has but recently come to my full attention. When the Jews of Trent were sentenced to death by Bishop Johannes Hinderbach for the supposed killing of the boy Simon in one of the few ritual murder trials of the Italian Renaissance, the bishop was applauded in prose and in verse, in Latin and in the vernacular, by a number of humanists including Pomponio Leto and Bartolommeo Platina, whereas the only scholar who tried to defend the Jews, the papal commissioner Battista de' Giudici, Bishop of Ventimiglia, was a theologian with a Thomist background who was not devoid of humanist learning, but who wrote against Bruni and against Platina.[24] I do not wish to counter one exaggeration with the opposite one, as happens so often. I merely wish to illustrate my point that the lines between humanism and scholasticism in the fourteenth and fifteenth centuries were not the same as the lines between liberalism and reaction in the eighteenth or nineteenth or even in the twentieth century.

So far I have spoken only of early Italian humanism and its own achievement. I can be shorter on my second major point, its influence outside of Italy, since I have dealt with this subject in another paper.[25] However, this is a large and complex subject that would require much further elaboration than I could give it in this paper or in my earlier paper. I am quite ready to grant that Renaissance humanism as it appears outside of Italy differs in many ways from the Italian variety, as a result of national traditions or of novel developments. Nevertheless, there is no doubt that by the sixteenth century, Italian

131

humanism had penetrated more or less deeply most of Western Europe from Spain and Portugal to Sweden and Poland, from France and England to Bohemia and Hungary. Foreign students and other visitors in Italy became acquainted with the humanists and their writings, went home with new books and interests, and remained in correspondence with their Italian friends and colleagues. Italian scholars and diplomats stayed abroad for shorter or longer periods and left behind a circle of friends and admirers. In this way, many manuscripts containing the writings of Italian humanists found their way into foreign libraries during the fifteenth and sixteenth centuries, and many humanist texts have been preserved for us only through such foreign copies. After the invention of printing and its introduction to Italy, several Italian cities, and especially Venice, became leading centers of the book trade, just as Florence had been a center of that trade during the late manuscript age, and the humanist editions published in Italy soon reached many foreign libraries. Before long, numerous works of the Italian humanists were copied and reprinted abroad, and also translated into the various vernacular languages. The evidence is vast, and only a part of it has been collected, but even the available information is fairly extensive, especially for France, the Low Countries, and the German-speaking countries, but also for Spain and England, Poland and Hungary. To cite but a few examples that may be less commonly known, I found in Portugal a Portuguese translation of Quintus Curtius based on the Italian version of Pier Candido Decembrio,[26] and in Sweden a group of humanist manuscripts collected by a fifteenth-century bishop who had studied at Perugia.[27] The cathedral library of a small town in Northern Castile has a group of more than twenty humanist manuscripts, some of them containing great rarities, that come again from a fifteenth-century bishop who had spent some time in Italy.[28]

Of even greater importance than these foreign traces of Italian activities is the rise of a genuine humanism outside of Italy, original and with local roots, but clearly influenced by Italian models and precedents. It appears wherever we find local scholars who show in their work the pattern of humanist learning, or to be more modest and more factual, wherever we find the humanist script and the study of Greek. Petrarch had his pupils in Bohemia and in France as well as in Italy,[29] and Enea Silvio Piccolomini had many friends and admirers in Austria and in Germany.[30] Matthias Corvinus of Hungary called many Italian scholars to his court and collected their writings in his famous library.[31] Philippus Callimachus, who fled from Italy to Poland, came to occupy an important position at court and exercised great influence in his adopted country. By the end of the fifteenth century, Germany had produced Reuchlin and many lesser humanists; France, Fichet and Gaguin; and Spain, Nebrija. In the sixteenth century, Northern humanism gained momentum and began to challenge Italian supremacy. Erasmus, More and Budé were considering themselves at least the equals of their Italian contemporaries, if not of their predecessors, and by the middle of the sixteenth century, the center of Greek studies had moved to France, whereas the center of Latin studies by the end of the century had moved to the Low Countries. We might say without exaggeration that throughout the sixteenth century the contributions of the Italians to humanist learning were matched or surpassed by those of their foreign rivals, and that the study of the classics flourished as much in the West and North as it did in Italy.

The pattern of humanist learning as we have described it survived also the upheavals of the Protestant and Catholic reformations. Scholars of all areas and religious affiliations continued to produce editions, translations, and commentaries of classical writers, and to write Latin letters and speeches, and poems and dialogues on old and new themes. The work of these later writers is less widely known, and their reputation suffers from national and religious prejudices, and also from professional prejudices such as the contempt of the use of Latin professed by historians of modern literature. Yet a few scholars, such as Lipsius and Scaliger, or even in Italy, Sigonius and Victorius, are still famous for their classical learning. And one author of the late sixteenth century whom I should definitely claim as a late and distinguished Renaissance humanist is still famous in the annals of moral thought and of literature because he wrote in French: Michel de Montaigne.[32] The content, pattern, and style of his writing and thinking is thoroughly humanistic. He is imbued with the classical writers and cites them on nearly every page. His wisdom is drawn, not only from classical sources, but also from his personal experience and observation: he is a Renaissance individualist par excellence. The form of his essays, a new literary genre which he bequeathed to subsequent centuries, is much indebted to the traditions of humanist prose, especially to the letters and treatises of the humanists.

A movement that begins with Petrarch and ends with Montaigne is hardly in need of defenders, when its contribution to letters, to learning, and to thought, in Italy and in the rest of Europe, is subjected to serious scrutiny.

I come now to the third and most difficult part of my paper, in which I shall try to discuss as briefly as possible the impact of Renaissance humanism, both in Italy and elsewhere, on those areas of civilization that do not belong to the proper province of the humanists, the humanities. I shall not try to say much about the arts since others are better equipped to deal with this subject. In the case of literature, it is evident that much of the Latin writing of the humanists is literary in character. If we wish to limit the concept of literature to the vernacular, as many historians seem inclined to do, we must insist that many humanists were bilingual in their writings and also made important contributions to vernacular literature. The list includes not only Petrarch and Boccaccio, but Landino and Poliziano, Boiardo and Ariosto. Even Tasso possessed a considerable amount of humanist learning.[33] Yet the general impact of humanism on vernacular literature would be the subject of a very large discourse all by itself, involving such diverse aspects as themes, literary genres, and criteria of style. The impact of humanism on musical theory and practice is a difficult subject that has been recently treated by several musicologists,[34] and that may lend itself to further investigation. The influence of humanism on the visual arts has been explored by many art historians in recent years.[35] As a result of their studies, it seems safe to assert that the humanist enthusiasm for the study and imitation of classical antiquity had its counterpart in architecture and in sculpture; that it was the humanist climate of opinion that brought about the more frequent choice of themes from classical history and mythology in the painting of the fifteenth century and of the subsequent centuries; and that there was a growing number of theoretical treatises on the arts in which the professional experience of the artists was often combined with the classical learning of the humanists, especially when both were combined in the same person as in the case of Leon Battista Alberti.

Political thought, as we have seen, was considered a part of moral philosophy, and the early humanists from Salutati and Bruni down to Pontano contributed many treatises to this subject.[36] We might add Erasmus and More, and perhaps even Machiavelli.[37] He wrote in Tuscan rather than in Latin, to be sure, and some of his ideas are strikingly original, but it would be wrong to overlook the impact of classical learning on his work. He was deeply influenced by Polybius and Livy, and quite familiar with the political writings of Plato, Aristotle, and Cicero.

The impact of humanism on the mathematical disciplines is not yet sufficiently known. I should like to mention but a few established facts. Whereas Euclid and Ptolemy and even much of Archimedes were known in the Middle Ages,[38] such advanced authors as Pappus and Diophantus were first translated during the Renaissance.[39] I think we may say that additional ancient sources were of practical importance up to the moment when modern mathematics went beyond the knowledge possessed by the Greeks. This happened only during the sixteenth century, with the discovery of the solution of cubic equations. The work of Copernicus in astronomy was based on new observations and new thinking, to be sure, but he knew through literary testimonies of his ancient predecessors, and he was himself sufficiently trained as a humanist to translate an obscure Greek text into Latin.[40] The contribution of fifteenth-century Italy to astronomy, especially in the person of Giovanni Bianchini, is still largely unexplored, but it must not concern us in this paper, for in my terminology the history of astronomy as such is not a part of the history of humanism.

We might add a few similar remarks concerning medicine. The humanists contributed many new translations of Hippocrates, Galen, and other Greek medical writers, but the quantity and quality of these humanist translations, as compared with the medieval ones, has not yet been studied.[41] However, we might say that in medicine, just as in mathematics, it was important to absorb the entire patrimony of ancient knowledge before the moderns could go beyond it. The new discoveries made in anatomy and other fields by Vesalius and others were due to fresh observations, but it might be argued that such observations were encouraged by the humanist critique of medieval authorities.[42]

The humanist contribution to jurisprudence and especially to the study of Roman law has been investigated by several recent scholars.[43] The direct study of the *Corpus Juris* had been revived at Bologna in the twelfth century and had spread from there to other centers in Italy, France, and other countries. This study was, and remained for several centuries, scholastic and dialectical in its method. In the fifteenth century, and under the influence of humanism, scholars who were not professional jurists, such as Valla, Vegio, and Poliziano, began to apply the methods of historical and philological criticism to the *Corpus Juris*. By the end of the fifteenth century, some professional jurists, especially at Pavia, had begun to combine this method with the traditional one.[44] In the sixteenth century, the Frenchman Budé and the Italian Alciati, who was trained at Pavia but who taught for many years in France, fully developed this historical method which had many followers in Germany and Switzerland and especially in France. In jurisprudence this method became known as the *mos Gallicus*, although it had some of its roots in Italian humanism, whereas *mos Italicus* indicated the tradition of scholastic jurisprudence that continued to prevail at the Italian universities. The significance of this humanist jurisprudence in France and elsewhere seems to be a fertile field for much further study.[45] It involves not only the relations between legal theory and practice, but also the theory and methodology of history. It is no coincidence that many of the writers on the art of history who were active in the late sixteenth century were jurists from France.[46] Their list includes Jean Bodin, who was a humanist jurist and probably the most important political thinker after Machiavelli.

The relation of humanism to religious and theological thought is very complex, and we can hardly do justice to it in this brief summary. I should like to limit myself to a few observations. The often expressed view that theology was by definition scholastic and that humanism had no relevance to it is in need of serious qualifications. After the middle of the fifteenth century, many theologians in Italy and elsewhere had a humanist training.[47] At least one commentary on the *Sentences* was written in the humanist style, and another was written *ad mentem Platonis*.[48] The methods of historical and philological criticism which the humanists had developed in the study of the classical writers were capable of being applied to theological no less than to legal or scientific sources. Biblical scholarship owes much to humanists such as Valla and Erasmus, and we might add to them the work of Manetti, who is usually forgotten when this important subject is discussed.[49] The humanist contribution to patristic scholarship is largely ignored, but it is extensive and important. The editing and study of the Latin Fathers owes much to Erasmus and other humanists, whereas the editing and translating of the Greek Fathers was largely the work of Renaissance humanists, laymen and clerics, Italians and Northerners, Catholics and Protestants. The mere bibliographical record of this activity has not yet been established, and is rather hard to establish, but the article on Gregory Nazianzen prepared by Sister Agnes Clare Way for the *Catalogus Translationum et Commentariorum* will provide an important specimen for this kind of investigation that I hope will be followed by many others.[50] Only when this preliminary spadework has been far enough advanced will it be possible to raise the further question whether and to what extent the theological doctrines and debates of the sixteenth century were influenced by Greek patristic writings that had been unknown, or less widely known, during the preceding centuries. The impact of historical scholarship on the controversies of the Reformation period has been rightly emphasized in at least one substantial study.[51] We might add that Erasmus considered himself, and was considered by many of his contemporaries, to be a theologian among other things. The whole attitude of the Reformation period towards the sources of Christianity, that is, the tendency to go back beyond the Scholastics and their dialectic to the Bible and to the church fathers who still belong to the period of classical antiquity, reflects a fundamentally humanistic attitude. And since it is a widespread opinion that Italy in the fifteenth century was uninterested in religion and theology I should like to insist that fifteenth-century Italy produced a very large theological literature, and an even larger religious literature, written partly by laymen and partly by priests and monks, that is thoroughly imbued with humanist style and humanist learning, and that includes commentaries and questions, lives of saints and sermons, but also many treatises and dialogues.[52] This literature usually is not even mentioned by literary historians, and when it is mentioned, it is scorned rather than discussed. But it should be studied, for it illustrates a combination of attitudes and ideas usually considered incompatible, and its very existence, as is so often the case, disproves the validity of certain theories stubbornly repeated by those who wish to believe certain conventional views and refuse to modify them in the light of contrary evidence.

We finally come to the most important disciplines in which we want to assess the impact of humanism, or the lack of it, namely the philosophical disciplines other than ethics, including natural philosophy which in the terminology of the time contains several fields now treated as sciences. If we begin with the Aristotelian tradition that continued to dominate the teaching of philosophy, and the professional literature that grew out of this teaching, in Italy and elsewhere, it would be well to keep in mind the fact that the innovations in physics due to the Paris and Oxford nominalists of the fourteenth century came to form the core of instruction at the Italian universities from the late fourteenth to the end of the sixteenth century, and that the Italian schools were actually the chief centers of transmission for these doctrines during the entire period.[53] If Leonardo and Galileo were familiar with Parisian or Oxonian physics, it was due to the teaching and writing of their Italian masters who assiduously transmitted, discussed, and perhaps developed these doctrines. This tradition coexisted throughout the Renaissance with Italian humanism, even at the universities themselves, and was but slightly affected by it. To say that Italian humanism retarded the progress of physics for two centuries is completely pointless,[54] for the humanists operated in entirely different areas of learning, and the Italian Aristotelians kept the Northern tradition in physics very much alive at the same time — unless we wish to deplore the fact that Galileo did not arise two hundred years before his time, a kind of lament that is as easy as it is futile. The case of Renaissance physics is a major example, though not the only one, for our contention that humanism constitutes an important sector of Renaissance civilization, but by no means the only one. On the other hand, Leonardo was not so completely untouched by humanism as is often asserted.[55]

Another science that was treated as a part of natural philosophy was what we call biology. Zoology continued to be treated on the basis of Aristotle, whereas botany was very much enriched by the newly translated works of Theophrastus.[56] In the sixteenth century these fields profited much from new observations, and especially from the study of new plants and animals found in the New World.[57]

Another discipline in which the Renaissance universities continued and perhaps developed the traditions of the fourteenth century was logic, and especially terminist logic. Again, this contribution has not yet been sufficiently studied, and the impact of humanism seems to have been rather slight. However, we do encounter cases of scholars who were interested both in logic and in the humanities.[58] There were also important attempts to reform logic from a humanist point of view that emphasized its connection with rhetoric. This tendency began with Valla, was continued by Agricola and others, and reached a climax with Peter Ramus, who succeeded in founding a new school of logic that competed with the Aristotelian school even at some universities and survived for a long time. This new trend in logic which is clearly of humanistic origin has been variously judged by modern historians. Its contribution to formal logic seems to have been slight, but significantly this logic was concerned with the tasks of teaching and learning and with the methods most appropriate for a clear exposition of a subject.[59]

When we finally consider the central philosophical disciplines of metaphysics and cosmology during our period, we must again begin with the Aristotelian tradition that predominated at the universities. Renaissance Aristotelianism was quite vigorous, and it continued in many ways the traditions of the thirteenth and fourteenth centuries.[60] Yet it gradually underwent some changes, especially during the sixteenth century, and at least some of these changes may be attributed to the influence of humanism. The humanists cultivated the study of the Greek text of

Aristotle, and they supplied new translations of Aristotle that altered the terminology and gradually replaced the older ones as university textbooks.[61] Moreover, many of the ancient Greek commentaries on Aristotle were made available for the first time through humanist translations.[62] Finally, the remainder of Greek philosophical literature outside the Aristotelian school became generally available, and I cannot agree with those of my medievalist colleagues who consider this literature as unimportant. Also the knowledge of Greek, the new literary style and the emphasis on certain new problems made themselves felt. I should not be inclined to call Pomponazzi a humanist, for he knew no Greek, and his style is entirely scholastic. Yet he cites Greek authors unknown to his medieval predecessors, such as Plato or Plutarch; he borrows important doctrines not only from Alexander of Aphrodisias but also from the Stoics; and he is interested in such fashionable problems as fate and fortune, the immortality of the soul, or the dignity of man. Of some later Aristotelians such as Jacopo Zabarella we may justly say that they had completely absorbed what humanism had to offer to an Aristotelian philosopher: he knew Greek, wrote a smooth Latin style, and was familiar with all philosophical sources of antiquity.

However, it would be misleading to suggest that the history of Renaissance metaphysics was limited to the Aristotelianism taught at the universities. Some of the most powerful and influential thinkers fall outside this scheme. Nicolaus Cusanus derives many of his central doctrines from Northern mysticism, and he is strongly affected by Greek Platonist sources, some of them first translated in his time or even for his use.[63] His style and orientation are neither scholastic nor humanistic,[64] but his personal contacts and his library show that he was much closer to Italian humanism than is often asserted.[65] Ficino and Pico are often claimed as humanists, and there is a strong humanist element in their background and work: Ficino's activity as a translator and commentator owes much to humanist antecedents, and Pico's oriental studies follow the precedent of Manetti. I prefer to treat them as philosopher-humanists, if I may be permitted to use this term, that is, as thinkers who combine the professional traditions of philosophy with humanist learning, just as Alciati did in jurisprudence and others in medicine or theology. Yet even if we do not consider Ficino and Pico as straight humanists, their work is unthinkable without humanism, and this includes their restatement of ancient Platonist doctrine.[66]

The philosophers of nature of the sixteenth century, such as Telesio, Patrizi, or Bruno, were primarily concerned with supplying new alternatives to the traditional cosmology and metaphysics of the Aristotelian school. They were original, speculative philosophers, and I think they deserve the name of humanists even less than Cusanus, let alone Ficino or Pico. They were all more or less affected by their humanist background: in their literary style, in their command of ancient sources, and occasionally in their emphasis on certain themes or problems. Yet when we look at Renaissance philosophy as a whole in the sixteenth and even in the fifteenth century, it seems evident to me that we cannot identify it with humanism, and that we must treat humanism merely as one of the ingredients that contributed to the development of philosophical thought during our period.

I shall forego the temptation to state what Galileo and Descartes, what early modern philosophy and science owe to Renaissance thought, and especially to Renaissance humanism. I merely wish to repeat that in my opinion early Italian humanism was an important and influential movement that had a great and pervasive impact on the thought and learning of its own time and of subsequent centuries. It originated as a literary and scholarly movement with strong interests in moral problems, and not as a philosophical movement in the technical or modern sense of the term. It made great contributions to the study of the classics and to other related branches of learning. It also contributed to the history of thought including philosophy, theology, and the sciences, but these contributions were largely of an indirect nature, involving such matters as methods and style, sources and themes, and for the most part they came about at a comparatively late period, after the middle of the fifteenth century, and through significant compromises between humanism and the various professional and technical traditions of the later Middle Ages.

If we compare the state of thought and learning in the early fourteenth and in the early seventeenth century, Renaissance humanism fills a part of the gap. It supplied the foundations on which modern historical, philological, and literary scholarship have developed. It also contributed to modern philosophy and thought to the extent to which the latter depends on the ancient philosophical sources made available and interpreted by this scholarship. Within the context of the Renaissance, the impact of humanism was greater than it may appear from a modern perspective. For the role of the humanities, and of classical scholarship, was much greater than it is now, and this is not only due to a literary or educational fashion, but also to the fact that classical antiquity supplied to the Renaissance a body of literary masterpieces that had not been sufficiently known or appreciated before, and a body of philosophical and scientific learning that had not yet been completely absorbed, let alone surpassed. The time when the West began to surpass the ancients in the sciences and perhaps in philosophy did not come until the middle of the sixteenth century. The belief that we also surpass the ancients in the arts and in literature is of much more recent date, and we may wonder at times whether or not it is justified.

BY PAUL OSKAR KRISTELLER

NOTES

1. P. O. Kristeller, *Studies in Renaissance Thought and Letters* (Rome, 1956); *Renaissance Thought* (New York, 1961); "Studies on Renaissance Humanism during the Last Twenty Years," *Studies in the Renaissance*, IX (1962), 7-30; "Changing Views of the Intellectual History of the Renaissance since Jacob Burckhardt," in *The Renaissance*, ed. Tinsley Helton (Madison, Wisc., 1961), 27-52; *Eight Philosophers of the Italian Renaissance* (Stanford, Cal., 1964); *Renaissance Thought II* (New York, 1965); *Renaissance Philosophy and the Medieval Tradition* (Latrobe, Pa., 1966); "Philosophy and Humanism in Renaissance Perspective," in *The Renaissance Image of Man and the World*, ed. Bernard O'Kelley (Columbus, O., 1966), pp. 29-51. In addition to the literature referred to below, see also A. Buck, *Die humanistische Tradition in der Romania* (Bad Homburg, 1968); C. Dionisotti, *Discorso sull'umanesimo italiano* (Verona, 1956); G. Saitta, *Il pensiero italiano nell'Umanesimo e nel Rinascimento*, 3 vols. (Bologna, 1949-51); Jerrold E. Seigel, *Rhetoric and Philosophy in Renaissance Humanism* (Princeton, N.J., 1968); C. J. de Vogel, *Het Humanisme* (Assen, 1968).

2. F. Masai, "La notion de Renaissance, Equivoques et malentendus," *Revue Belge d'Archéologie et d'Histoire de l'art*, XXXIV (1965), 137-66.

3. E. Garin, *Der Italienische Humanismus* (Bern, 1947); *L'umanesimo italiano* (Bari, 1952); *Italian Humanism*, tr. Peter Munz (New York, 1965); B. Nardi, *Saggi sull'Aristotelismo Padovano dal secolo XIV al XVI* (Florence, 1958).

4. G. Tiraboschi, *Storia della letteratura italiana* (many editions); G. Voigt, *Die Wiederbelebung des classischen Alterthums*, 3rd ed. by M. Lehnerdt (Berlin, 1893); R. Sabbadini, *Le scoperte dei codici latini e greci ne' secoli XIV e XV*, 2 vols. (Florence, 1905-14); *Classici e umanisti da codici ambrosiani* (Florence, 1953).

5. K. Burdach, ed. *Vom Mittelalter zur Reformation*, 7 vols. (Berlin, 1912-39); A. Coville, *Gontier et Pierre Col et l'humanisme en France au temps de Charles VI* (Paris, 1934); Franco Simone, *Il Rinascimento francese* (Turin, 1961).

6. See my article, "Humanism and Scholasticism in the Italian Renaissance," in my *Renaissance Thought*, pp. 92-119 (1961, first published in 1945); A. Campana, "The Origin of the Word 'Humanist'," *Journal of the Warburg and Courtauld Institutes*, IX (1946), 60-73; P. Grendler, "Five Italian Occurrences of *Umanista*, 1540-1574," *Renaissance Quarterly*, XX (1967), 317-26. In a forthcoming article, Professor Grendler will discuss some more instances of the use of the term *umanista*.

7. On the use of the term in Salutati, see Eckhard Kessler, *Das Problem des frühen Humanismus* (Munich, 1968).

8. P. O. Kristeller, "Il Petrarca, l'Umanesimo e la Scolastica a Venezia," in *La Civiltà Veneziana del Trecento* (Florence, 1956), pp. 147-78.

9. G. Billanovich, *I primi umanisti e le tradizioni dei classici latini* (Fribourg, 1953); B. L. Ullman, *Studies in the Italian Renaissance* (Rome, 1955); R. Weiss, *The Dawn of Humanism in Italy* (London, 1947); *Il primo secolo dell'umanesimo*

(Rome, 1949); G. Billanovich, F. Čadá, A. Campana, P. O. Kristeller, "Scuola di Retorica e poesia bucolica nel Trecento Italiano," *Italia Medioevale e Umanistica,* IV (1961), 181-221.

10. H. Wieruszowski, "Rhetoric and the Classics in Italian Education of the Thirteenth Century," *Collectanea Stephan Kuttner,* I, in *Studia Gratiana,* XI (Bologna, 1967), 169-207. A recent attempt to question the authenticity of Dante's Latin poems to Giovanni del Virgilio by Aldo Rossi, "Dante, Boccaccio e la laurea poetica," *Paragone,* XIII (1962), 3-41, has not met with general acceptance.

11. Q. Breen, "Giovanni Pico della Mirandola on the Conflict of Philosophy and Rhetoric," *Journal of the History of Ideas,* XIII (1952), 384-426; reprinted as "Three Renaissance Humanists on the Relation of Philosophy and Rhetoric," in his *Christianity and Humanism,* ed. Nelson Peter Ross (Grand Rapids, Mich., 1968), pp. 1-68.

12. B. L. Ullman, *The Origin and Development of Humanistic Script* (Rome, 1960).

13. Vittorio Rossi, *Il Quattrocento,* 8th ed. by Aldo Vallone (Milan, 1964).

14. J. E. Sandys, *A History of Classical Scholarship,* 3 vols. (Cambridge, 1908-21); see also the works of Sabbadini (above, note 4).

15. For the medieval background of the humanist study of Greek, see R. Devreesse, *Les manuscrits grecs de l'Italie méridionale* (Vatican City, 1955); A. Pertusi, *Leonzio Pilato fra Petrarca e Boccaccio* (Venice, 1964); Kenneth M. Setton, "The Byzantine Background to the Italian Renaissance," *Proceedings of the American Philosophical Society,* C (1956), 1-76.

16. Sesto Prete, "Leistungen der Humanisten auf dem Gebiete der lateinischen Philologie," *Philologus,* CIX (1965), 259-69.

17. *Catalogus Translationum et Commentariorum: Mediaeval and Renaissance Latin Translations and Commentaries,* I, ed. P. O. Kristeller (Washington, D.C., 1960); the second volume will appear in the near future.

18. Leonardo Aretino Bruni, *Humanistisch-Philosophische Schriften,* ed. H. Baron (Leipzig, 1928); J. Soudek, "Leonardo Bruni and His Public: A Statistical and Interpretative Study of His Annotated Latin Version of the (Pseudo-) Aristotelian Economics," *Studies in Medieval and Renaissance History,* V (1968), 49-136.

19. E. Garin, *Der italienische Humanismus* (Bern, 1947); *Il pensiero pedagogico dello umanesimo* (Florence, 1958); *Storia della filosofia italiana,* 3 vols. (Turin, 1966); *La cultura filosofica del Rinascimento italiano* (Florence, 1961).

20. H. Baron, *The Crisis of the Early Italian Renaissance,* 2 vols. (Princeton, N.J., 1955; rev. ed. in one vol., 1966); *Humanistic and Political Literature in Florence and Venice at the Beginning of the Quattrocento* (Cambridge, Mass., 1955); *From Petrarch to Leonardo Bruni* (Chicago, 1968); Eugene F. Rice, *The Renaissance Idea of Wisdom* (Cambridge, Mass., 1958); Charles Trinkaus, *Adversity's Noblemen* (New York, 1940). See also the studies by Garin (above note 19).

148

21. An edition of the three treatises by Lauro Quirini on the subject is being prepared by Dr. Helmut Roob and Dr. Konrad Krautter.

22. Tristano Caracciolo, *Nobilitatis neapolitanae defensio,* published among his *Opuscula historica* in *Rerum Italicarum Scriptores,* XXII, ed. L. A. Muratori (Milan, 1733), coll. 121-28, and in *Raccolta di tutti i più rinomati scrittori dell'istoria generale del regno di Napoli* (Naples, 1769), VI, 152-60. Cf. M. Santoro, *Tristano Caracciolo e la Cultura Napoletana della Rinascenza* (Naples, 1957), pp. 137-64.

23. *Prose e rime de' due Buonaccorsi da Montemagno* (Florence, 1718), pp. 1-96. The text found in E. Garin, *Prosatori latini del Quattrocento* (Milan, 1952), pp. 141-65, is incomplete.

24. P. O. Kristeller, *Le thomisme et la pensée italienne de la Renaissance* (Montreal, 1967), p. 68. The literary history of this sad episode remains to be written. Several compositions by Zovenzonius, Tiberinus, Cimbriacus, and others are found in early printed editions, many others in Capsa 69 of the Archivio Principesco Vescovile in the Archivio di Stato at Trent.

25. "The European Diffusion of Italian Humanism," in my *Renaissance Thought II,* pp. 69-88.

26. Lisbon, Biblioteca de Ajuda, ms. 52 VII 3.

27. "The European Diffusion," p. 81. H. Aminson, *Bibliotheca Templi Cathedralis Strengnesensis, Supplementum* (Stockholm, 1863), pp. i-lix.

28. T. Rojo Orcajo, *Catálogo descriptivo de los Códices que se conservan en la santa iglesia catedral de Burgo de Osma* (Madrid, 1929). The manuscripts were kindly shown to me in May, 1968, by D. José Arranz, Canonigo Archivero. They include texts by Mussato, Bruni, Poggio, Traversari, Cincius Romanus, Trapezuntius, Pius II, Johannes Tintus of Fabriano, Franciscus Aretinus, Decembrio, Omnibonus Leonicenus, Lorenzo Bonincontri, and Marsilio Ficino.

29. See above, note 5.

30. Pius II, *Briefwechsel,* ed. R. Wolkan, 4 vols. (Vienna, 1908-18); *Ausgewählte Texte,* ed. B. Widmer (Basel, 1960); B. Widmer, *Enea Silvio Piccolomini in der sittlichen und politischen Entscheidung* (Basel, 1963); A. Lhotsky, *Aeneas Silvius und Österreich* (Basel, 1965); G. Kisch, *Enea Silvio Piccolomini und die Jurisprudenz* (Basel, 1967).

31. G. Fraknoi, *et al., Bibliotheca Corvina* (Budapest, 1927); A. De Hevesey, *La bibliothèque du roi Matthias Corvin* (Paris, 1923).

32. Donald M. Frame, *Montaigne's Discovery of Man* (New York, 1955).

33. See the literary histories of Tiraboschi and V. Rossi, and G. Toffanin, *Il Cinquecento,* 7th ed. (Milan, 1965). See also C. Dionisotti, *Gli Umanisti e il Volgare fra Quattro e Cinquecento* (Florence, 1968).

34. D. P. Walker, "Musical Humanism in the 16th and early 17th Centuries," *The Music Review,* II (1941), 1-13, 111-21, 220-27, 288-308; III (1942), 55-71; *Der musikalische Humanismus im 16. und fruehen 17. Jahrhundert* (Kassel and Basel, 1949); G. Reese, *Music in the Renaissance* (New York, 1954; rev. ed., 1959); E. Lowinsky, "Music in the Culture of the Renaissance," *Journal of the History*

of Ideas, XV (1954), 509-53, repr. in *Renaissance Essays*, ed. P. O. Kristeller and P. P. Wiener (New York, 1968), 337-81; "Music of the Renaissance as Viewed by the Musicians," in *The Renaissance Image of Man and the World*, pp. 129-77.

35. A. Chastel, *Art et humanisme à Florence au temps de Laurent le Magnifique* (Paris, 1961); E. H. Gombrich, "Botticelli's Mythologies: A Study in the Neoplatonic Symbolism of his Circle," *Journal of the Warburg and Courtauld Institutes*, VIII (1945), 7-60; "*Icones Symbolicae:* The Visual Image in Neo-Platonic Thought," *ibid.*, XI (1948), 163-92; H. W. Janson, "The Image of Man in Renaissance Art: From Donatello to Michelangelo," in *The Renaissance Image of Man and the World*, pp. 77-103; M. Meiss, *Andrea Mantegna as Illuminator* (New York, 1957); E. Panofsky, *Idea* (Leipzig, 1924; 2nd ed., Berlin, 1960); tr. Joseph J. S. Peake (Columbia, S.C., 1968); *Studies in Iconology* (New York, 1939); *Meaning in the Visual Arts* (Garden City, N.Y., 1955); F. Saxl, *Lectures*, 2 vols. (London, 1957); W. Stechow, *Rubens and the Classics* (Cambridge, Mass., 1968); E. Wind, *Pagan Mysteries in the Renaissance* (New Haven, 1958; rev. ed., London, 1968); R. Wittkower, *Architectural Principles in the Age of Humanism* (London, 1949; 3rd rev. ed., 1962).

36. See the studies by Baron (above, note 20).

37. Felix Gilbert, *Machiavelli and Guicciardini* (Princeton, N.J., 1965).

38. M. Clagett, *Archimedes in the Middle Ages* (Madison, Wisc., 1964).

39. See the forthcoming article on Pappus by Marjorie Boyer (to appear in vol. II of the *Catalogus Translationum et Commentariorum*).

40. Theophylactus Simocatta, *Epistolae*, tr. Nicolaus Copernicus (Cracow, 1509): G. W. Panzer, *Annales Typographici:* (Nürnberg, 1793-1803), VI, 452, no. 33; a modern facsimile edition was published in Warsaw, 1953.

41. P. Kibre, "Hippocratic Writings in the Middle Ages," *Bulletin of the History of Medicine*, XVIII (1945), 371-412; R. Durling, "A Chronological Census of Renaissance Editions and Translations of Galen," *Journal of the Warburg and Courtauld Institutes*, XXIV (1961), 230-305.

42. L. Edelstein, "Andreas Vesalius, the Humanist," *Bulletin of the History of Medicine*, XIV (1943), 547-61.

43. M. P. Gilmore, *Humanists and Jurists* (Cambridge, Mass., 1963); D. Maffei, *Gli inizi dell'umanesimo giuridico* (Milan, 1956); G. Kisch, *Humanismus und Jurisprudenz* (Basel, 1955); *Erasmus und die Jurisprudenz seiner Zeit* (Basel, 1960).

44. V. Lublinsky, "Le *Semideus* de Caton Sacco," *Analecta Medii Aevi*, II (Leningrad, 1927), 95-118; *Catonis Sacci Originum Liber Primus in Aristotelem*, ed. F. Adorno, *Rinascimento*, 2nd Ser. II (anno XIII, 1962), 157-95; III (anno XIV, 1963), 221-50; F. Gabotto, *Giason del Maino e gli scandali universitari nel Quattrocento* (Turin, 1888).

45. Donald R. Kelley, *Foundations of Modern Historical Scholarship* (forthcoming); "Legal Humanism and the Sense of History," *Studies in the Renaissance*, XIII (1966), 184-99; "Guillaume Budé and the First Historical School of Law," *American Historical Review*, LXII (1967), 807-34.

46. B. Reynolds, "Shifting Currents in Historical Criticism," *Journal of the History of Ideas*, XIV (1953), 471-92, repr. in *Renaissance Essays*, pp. 115-36.

47. P. O. Kristeller, *Le Thomisme et la pensée italienne de la Renaissance* (Montreal, 1967); "Sebastiano Salvini, a Florentine Humanist and Theologian, and a Member of Marsilio Ficino's Platonic Academy," in *Didascaliae, Studies in Honor of Anselm M. Albareda*, ed. S. Prete (New York, 1961), pp. 205-43; "An Unknown Humanist Sermon on St. Stephen by Guillaume Fichet," in *Mélanges Eugène Tisserant*, VI, *Studi e Testi*, CCXXXVI (Vatican City, 1964), 459-97.

48. The former by Paolo Cortesi, the latter by Giles of Viterbo. See F. Stegmüller, *Repertorium Commentariorum in Sententias Petri Lombardi* (Würzburg, 1947), I, 298-99, and 22-23; E. Massa, *I fondamenti metafisici della 'dignitas hominis'* (Turin, 1954), pp. 49-110; John W. O'Malley, *Giles of Viterbo on Church and Reform* (Leyden, 1968), p. 197.

49. S. Garofalo, "Gli umanisti italiani del secolo XV e la Bibbia," *Biblica*, XXVII (1946), 338-75, repr. in *La Bibbia e il Concilio di Trento* (Rome, 1947), pp. 38-75.

50. See above, note 17.

51. P. Polman, *L'élément historique dans la controverse religieuse du XVIe siècle* (Gembloux, 1932).

52. See above, note 47; H. Jedin, "Studien über Domenico de' Domenichi," *Akademie der Wissenschaften und der Literatur, Mainz, Abhandlungen der Geistes- und Sozialwissenschaftlichen Klasse*, V (1957), 175-300.

· 53. P. Duhem, *Etudes sur Léonard de Vinci*, 3 vols. (Paris, 1906-13); A. Koyré, *Etudes Galiléennes*, 3 vols. (Paris, 1939); M. Clagett, *Giovanni Marliani and Late Medieval Physics* (New York, 1941); Curtis Wilson, *William Heytesbury* (Madison, Wisc., 1956); Anneliese Maier, *Studien zur Naturphilosophie der Spätscholastik*, 5 vols. (Rome, 1949-58); *Ausgehendes Mittelalter*, 2 vols. (Rome, 1964-67); E. Rosen, "Renaissance Science as Seen by Burckhardt and his Successors," in *The Renaissance*, ed. Tinsley Helton (Madison, Wisc., 1961), pp. 77-103; J. H. Randall, *The School of Padua and the Emergence of Modern Science* (Padua, 1961); *The Career of Philosophy*, I: *From the Middle Ages to the Enlightenment* (New York, 1962).

54. A. Crombie, *Augustine to Galileo* (London, 1952, and later editions); cf. G. Sarton, *The Appreciation of Ancient and Medieval Science during the Renaissance* (Philadelphia, 1955); L. Thorndike, *A History of Magic and Experimental Science*, 8 vols. (New York, 1923-58).

55. L. Reti, "The Two Unpublished Manuscripts of Leonardo Da Vinci in the Biblioteca Nacional of Madrid," *Burlington Magazine*, CX (1968), 10-22, 81-87.

56. The article on Theophrastus for the *Catalogus Translationum et Commentariorum* is being prepared by Charles B. Schmitt.

57. The article on Strabo for the *Catalogus Translationum* is being prepared by

Aubrey Diller. For discussion of the translation of Ptolemy's *Geography* by Jacopo Angeli da Scarperia, see Joseph Fischer, *Tomus Prodromus, Claudii Ptolemaei Geographiae codex Urbinas graecus 82* (Leyden, 1932). Cf. E. Garin, *Scienza e vita civile nel Rinascimento italiano* (Bari, 1965).

58. Pietro Alboini da Mantova, Pier Paolo Vergerio, who taught logic at Padua, and Ermolao Barbaro. For Pietro Alboini da Mantova, see Coluccio Salutati, *Epistolario*, ed. F. Novati, III (Rome, 1896), pp. 319-20; C. Vasoli, "Pietro degli Alboini da Mantova 'scolastico' della Fine del Trecento e un' Epistola di Coluccio Salutati," *Rinascimento*, 2nd Ser., III (anno XIV, 1963), 3-21, repr. in *Arte Pensiero e Cultura a Mantova nel primo Rinascimento in Rapporto con la Toscana e con il Veneto* (Florence, 1965), pp. 57-75; and also Theodore James, ed., "De primo et ultimo instanti Petri Alboini Mantuani" (unpublished doctoral dissertation, Columbia University, 1968). For Pier Paolo Vergerio, see his *Epistolario*, ed. L. Smith (Rome, 1934), pp. xv and 484. For Ermolao Barbaro, see his *Epistolae, Orationes et Carmina*, ed. V. Branca (Florence, 1943), I, 87-90, 100-16; II, 22-23; cf. C. Dionisotti, "Ermolao Barbaro e la fortuna di Suiseth," in *Medioevo e Rinascimento, Studi in onore di Bruno Nardi*, I (Florence, 1955), 217-53.

59. C. Prantl, *Geschichte der Logik im Abendlande*, 4 vols. (Leipzig, 1855-70); Walter J. Ong, *Ramus: Method and the Decay of Dialogue* (Cambridge, Mass., 1958); Neal W. Gilbert, *Renaissance Concepts of Method* (New York, 1960); W. Risse, *Die Logik der Neuzeit* (Stuttgart, 1964); C. Vasoli, *La dialettica e la rettorica dell'Umanesimo* (Milan, 1968). See also the article by Breen (above, note II).

60. P. O. Kristeller, *La tradizione aristotelica nel Rinascimento* (Padua, 1962); "Renaissance Aristotelianism," *Greek, Roman and Byzantine Studies* (1965), VI, 157-74; see also the studies by Randall (above note 53).

61. P. O. Kristeller, "Un codice padovano di Aristotele postillato da Francesco ed Ermolao Barbaro," in my *Studies in Renaissance Thought and Letters*, pp. 337-53 (first published in 1948); see also the study by Soudek (above, note 18).

62. P. O. Kristeller, "Un codice padovano . . ."; F. E. Cranz, "Alexander Aphrodisiensis," in *Catalogus Translationum et Commentariorum*, I, 77-135.

63. R. Klibansky, "Plato's *Parmenides* in the Middle Ages and the Renaissance," *Mediaeval and Renaissance Studies*, I (1941-43), 281-330. I shall deal with the subject in a forthcoming article. The Greek texts translated for Cusanus include Plato's *Parmenides*, Albinus's *Isagoge*, Proclus's *Platonic Theology*, and Pletho's *De Fato*.

64. In the dialogue *Idiota*, ed. L. Bauer (Heidelberg, 1937), the Philosophus stands for scholasticism, the Orator for humanism, and the Idiota for the author.

65. See my forthcoming article.

66. E. Garin, *Giovanni Pico della Mirandola* (Florence, 1937); P. O. Kristeller,

Il pensiero filosofico di Marsilio Ficino (Florence, 1953); "Florentine Platonism and its Relations with Humanism and Scholasticism," *Church History,* VIII (1939), 201-11; "Giovanni Pico della Mirandola and His Sources," in *L'opera e il pensiero di Giovanni Pico della Mirandola nella storia dell'umanesimo* (Florence, 1965), I, 35-133.

SELECTIVE BIBLIOGRAPHY

Baron, H. *The Crisis of the Early Italian Renaissance.* 2 vols. Princeton, N.J., 1955; rev. ed. in 1 vol., 1966.

————. *Humanistic and Political Literature in Florence and Venice at the Beginning of the Quattrocento.* Cambridge, Mass., 1955.

————. *From Petrarch to Leonardo Bruni.* Chicago, 1968.

Billanovich, G. *I primi umanisti e le tradizione dei classici latini.* Fribourg, 1953.

Breen, Q. "Giovanni Pico della Mirandola on the Conflict of Philosophy and Rhetoric," *Journal of the History of Ideas,* XIII (1952), 384-426.

Bruni, Leonardo Aretino. *Humanistisch-Philosophische Schriften,* ed. H. Baron. Leipzig, 1928.

Buck, A. *Die humanistische Tradition in der Romania.* Bad Homburg, 1968.

Burdach, K., ed. *Vom Mittelalter zur Reformation.* 7 vols. Berlin, 1912-39.

Campana, A. "The Origin of the Word 'Humanist'," *Journal of the Warburg and Courtauld Institutes,* IX (1946), 60-73.

Clagett, M. *Archimedes in the Middle Ages.* Madison, Wisc., 1964.

————. *Giovanni Marliani and Late Medieval Physics.* New York, 1941.

Chastel, A. *Art et humanisme à Florence au temps de Laurent le Magnifique.* Paris, 1961.

Coville, A. *Gontier et Pierre Col et l'humanisme en France au temps de Charles VI.* Paris, 1934.

Cranz, F. E. "Alexander Aphrodisiensis," in *Catalogus Translationum et Commentariorum,* I, ed. P. O. Kristeller (Washington, 1960), 77-135.

Crombie, A. *Augustine to Galileo.* London, 1952.

Devreesse, R. *Les manuscrits grecs de Il'talie méridionale.* Vatican City, 1955.

Dionisotti, C. *Discorso sull'umanesimo italiano.* Verona, 1956.

————. *Gli Umanisti e il Volgare fra Quattro e Cinquecento.* Florence, 1968.

Duhem, P. *Etudes sur Léonard de Vinci.* 3 vols. Paris, 1906-13.

Durling, R. "A Chronological Census of Renaissance Editions and Translations of Galen," *Journal of the Warburg and Courtauld Institutes,* XXIV (1961), 230-305.

Frame, Donald M. *Montaigne's Discovery of Man.* New York, 1955.

Garin, E. *La cultura filosofica del Rinascimento italiano.* Florence, 1961.

————. *Giovanni Pico della Mirandola.* Florence, 1937.

————. *Italian Humanism,* trans. Peter Munz. New York, 1965.

————. *Der italienische Humanismus.* Bern, 1947.

Garin, E. *Il pensiero pedagogico dello umanesimo.* Florence, 1958.

———. *Scienza e vita civile nel Rinascimento italiano.* Bari, 1965.

———. *Storia della filosofia italiana.* 3 vols. Turin, 1966.

———. *L'umanesimo italiano.* Bari, 1952.

Gilbert, Felix. *Machiavelli and Guicciardini.* Princeton, N.J., 1965.

Gilbert, Neal W. *Renaissance Concepts of Method.* New York, 1960.

Gilmore, M. P. *Humanists and Jurists.* Cambridge, Mass., 1963.

Gombrich, E. H. "Botticelli's Mythologies: A Study in the Neoplatonic Symbolism of his Circle," *Journal of the Warburg and Courtauld Institutes,* VIII (1945), 7-60.

———. "*Icones Symbolicae:* The Visual Image in Neo-Platonic Thought," *Journal of the Warburg and Courtauld Institutes,* XI (1948), 163-92.

Helton, Tinsley, ed. *The Renaissance.* Madison, Wisc., 1961.

Janson, H. W. "The Image of Man in Renaissance Art: From Donatello to Michelangelo," in *The Image of Man and the World,* ed., B. O'Kelley (Columbus, Ohio, 1966), 77-103.

Kelley, Donald R. "Guillaume Budé and the First Historical School of Law," *American Historical Review,* LXII (1967), 807-34.

———. "Legal Humanism and the Sense of History," *Studies in the Renaissance,* XIII (1966), 184-99.

Kessler, Eckhard. *Das Problem des frühen Humanismus.* Munich, 1968.

Kibre, P. "Hippocratic writings in the Middle Ages," *Bulletin of the History of Medicine,* XVIII (1945), 371-412.

Kisch, G. *Enea Silvio Piccolomini und die Jurisprudenz.* Basel, 1967.

———. *Erasmus und die Jurisprudenz seiner Zeit.* Basel, 1960.

———. *Humanismus und Jurisprudenz.* Basel, 1955.

Klibansky, R. "Plato's Parmenides in the Middle Ages and the Renaissance," *Medieval and Renaissance Studies,* I (1941-43), 281-330.

Koyré, A. *Etudes Galiléennes.* 3 vols. Paris, 1939.

Kristeller, P. O., ed. *Catalogus Translationum et Commentariorum: Mediaeval and Renaissance Latin Translations and Commentaries,* I. Washington, D.C., 1960.

———. "Changing Views of the Intellectual History of the Renaissance since Jacob Burckhardt," in *The Renaissance,* ed. Tinsley Helton (Madison, Wisc., 1961), pp. 27-52.

———. *Eight Philosophers of the Italian Renaissance.* Stanford, Cal., 1964.

———. "Florentine Platonism and its Relations with Humanism and Scholasticism," *Church History,* VIII (1939), 201-11.

———. "Giovanni Pico della Mirandola and His Sources," in *L'opera e il pensiero di Giovanni Pico della Mirandola,* (Florence, 1965) I, 35-133.

———. *Il pensiero filosofico di Marsilio Ficino.* Florence, 1953.

———. "Il Petrarca, L'Umanesimo e la Scolastica a Venezia," in *La Civiltà Veneziana del Trecento* (Florence, 1956), pp. 147-78.

———. "Philosophy and Humanism in Renaissance Perspective," in *The*

Renaissance Image of Man and the World, ed. Bernard O'Kelley (Columbus, O.,
1966), pp. 29-51.

Kristeller, P. O. *The Philosophy of Marsilio Ficino*, trans. Virginia Conant. New
York, 1943.

———. *Renaissance Philosophy and the Medieval Tradition*. Latrobe, Pa., 1966.

———. *Renaissance Thought*. New York, 1961.

———. *Renaissance Thought II*. New York, 1965.

———. *Studies in Renaissance Thought and Letters*. Rome, 1956.

———. "Studies on Renaissance Humanism during the Last Twenty Years,"
Studies in the Renaissance, IX (1962), 7-30.

———. *Le Thomisme et la penseé italienne de la Renaissance*. Montreal, 1967.

———. *La tradizione aristotelica nel Rinascimento*. Padua, 1962.

———, and P. P. Wiener, eds. *Renaissance Essays*. New York, 1968.

Lowinsky, E. "Music in the Culture of the Renaissance," *Journal of the History
of Ideas*, XV (1954), 509-53.

———. "Music of the Renaissance as Viewed by the Musicians," in *The Image
of Man and the World*, ed. B. O'Kelley (Columbus Ohio, 1966), pp. 129-77.

Maffei, D. *Gli inizi dell'umanesimo giuridico*. Milan, 1956.

Maier, Anneliese. *Ausgehendes Mittelalter*. 2 vols. Rome, 1964-67.

———. *Studien zur Naturphilosophie der Spätscholastik*. 5 vols. Rome, 1949-58.

Masai, F. "La notion de Renaissance, Equivoques et malentendus," *Revue
Belge d'Archéologie et d'Histoire de l'art*, XXXIV (1965), 137-66.

Massa, E. *I fondamenti metafisici della 'dignitas hominis'*. Turin, 1954.

Meiss, M. *Andrea Mantegna as Illuminator*. New York, 1957.

Nardi, B. *Saggi sull'Aristotelismo Padovano dal secolo XIV al XVI*. Florence, 1958.

O'Kelley, Bernard, ed. *The Renaissance Image of Man and the World*. Columbus, O.,
1966.

O'Malley, John W. *Giles of Viterbo on Church and Reform*. Leyden, 1968.

Ong, Walter J. *Ramus: Method and the Decay of Dialogue*. Cambridge, Mass., 1958.

L'opera e il pensiero di Giovanni Pico della Mirandola nella storia dell'Umanesimo. 2
vols. Florence, 1965.

Panofsky, E. *Idea*. Leipzig, 1924. 2nd rev. ed., Berlin, 1960.

———. *Idea*. 2nd ed., trans. J. S. Peake. Columbia, S.C., 1968.

———. *Meaning in the Visual Arts*. Garden City, N.Y., 1955.

———. *Studies in Iconology*. New York, 1939.

Pertusi, A. *Leonzio Pilato fra Petrarca e Boccaccio*. Venice, 1964.

Polman, P. *L'élément historique dans la controverse religieuse du XVIᵉ siècle*. Gembloux,
1932.

Prantl, C. *Geschichte der Logik im Abendlande*. 4 vols. Leipzig, 1855-70.

Prete, Sesto. "Leistungen der Humanisten auf dem Gebiete der lateinischen
Philologie," *Philologus*, CIX (1965), 259-69.

Randall, J. H. *The Career of Philosophy*, I: *From the Middle Ages to the Enlightenment*.
New York, 1962.

Randall, J. H. *The School of Padua and the Emergence of Modern Science*. Padua, 1961.

Reese, G. *Music in the Renaissance*. Rev. ed. New York, 1959.

Reynolds, B. "Shifting Currents in Historical Criticism," *Journal of the History of Ideas*, XIV (1953), 471-92.

Rice, E. F. *The Renaissance Idea of Wisdom*. Cambridge, Mass., 1958.

Risse, W. *Die Logik der Neuzeit*. Stuttgart, 1964.

Rosen, E. "Renaissance Science as Seen by Burckhardt and His Successors," in *The Renaissance*, ed. Tinsley Helton (Madison, Wisc., 1961), pp. 77-103.

Rossi, Vittorio. *Il Quattrocento*. 8th ed. by Aldo Vallone. Milan, 1964.

Sabbadini, R. *Classici e umanisti da codici ambrosiani*. Florence, 1933.

———. *Le scoperte dei codici latini e greci ne' secoli XIV e XV*. 2 vols. Florence, 1905-14.

Saitta, G. *Il pensiero italiano nell'Umanesimo e nel Rinascimento*. 3 vols. Bologna, 1949-51.

Sandys, J. E. *A History of Classical Scholarship*. 3 vols. Cambridge, 1908-21.

Santoro, M. *Tristano Caracciolo e la cultura napoletana della Rinascenza*. Naples, 1957.

Sarton, G. *The Appreciation of Ancient and Medieval Science during the Renaissance*. Philadelphia, 1955.

Saxl, F. *Lectures*. 2 vols. London, 1957.

Seigel, Jerrold E. *Rhetoric and Philosophy in Renaissance Humanism*. Princeton, N.J., 1968.

Setton, K. M. "The Byzantine Background to the Italian Renaissance," *Proceedings of the American Philosophical Society*, C (1956), 1-76.

Simone, Franco. *Il Rinascimento francese*. Turin, 1961.

Soudek, J. "Leonardo Bruni and His Public: A Statistical and Interpretative Study of His Annotated Latin Version of the (Pseudo) Aristotelian Economics," *Studies in Medieval and Renaissance History*, V (1968), 49-136.

Stechow, W. *Rubens and the Classics*. Cambridge, Mass., 1968.

Thorndike, L. *A History of Magic and Experimental Science*. 8 vols. New York, 1923-58.

Toffanin, G. *Il Cinquecento*. 7th ed. Milan, 1965.

Trinkaus, C. *Adversity's Noblemen*. New York, 1941.

———. *"In Our Image and Likeness": Humanity and Divinity in Italian Humanist Thought*. 2 vols. Chicago, 1970.

Ullman, B. L. *The Origin and Development of Humanistic Script*. Rome, 1960.

Vasoli, C. *La dialettica e la rettorica dell'Umanesimo*. Milan, 1968.

Vogel, C. J. de. *Het Humanisme*. Assen, 1968.

Voigt, G. *Die Wiederbelebung des classischen Altertums*. 3rd ed. by M. Lehnerdt. Berlin, 1893.

Walker, D. P. *Der musikalische Humanismus im 16. und fruehen 17. Jahrhundert*. Kassel and Basel, 1949.

———. "Musical Humanism in the 16th and early 17th Centuries," *The*

Music Review, II (1941), 1-13; 111-21, 220-27, 288-308; III (1942), 55-71.

Weiss, R. *The Dawn of Humanism in Italy*. London, 1947.

———. *Il primo secolo dell'umanesimo*. Rome, 1949.

Widmer, B. *Enea Silvio Piccolomini in der sittlichen und politischen Entscheidung*. Basel, 1963.

Wieruszowski, Helene. "Rhetoric and the Classics in Italian Education of the Thirteenth Century," *Collectanea Stephan Kuttner*, I (*Studia Gratiana* XI, Bologna, 1967), 169-207.

Wilson, Curtis. *William Heytesbury*. Madison, Wisc., 1956.

Wind, E. *Pagan Mysteries in the Renaissance*. Rev. ed. London, 1968.

Wittkower, R. *Architectural Principles in the Age of Humanism*. 3rd rev. ed. London, 1962.

The Transformation of the Liberal Arts in the Renaissance

The history of culture is the sequence of man's accomplishments, recorded, ordered, distinguished into strands, and divided into stages. Since the conception of culture and of the history of culture is a part of that history, histories of culture change with the changes of culture, and at each stage of that history the sequence, the stages, and the strands of culture will be viewed and set forth according to the perspectives and conceptions then in vogue. At the next stage the culture of that period and its conceptions of the history of culture will in turn be analyzed and described in the new styles of the new period. Histories of culture are accounts of what men have made and thought and said: what has been conceived to be the cultural achievements or degradations of the past has influence on present attitudes and activities, and present values and interests determine what aspects of the past should be considered and how they should be judged. Histories of culture tend therefore to be accounts of battles of books, of the ancients and the moderns, in which cultural changes can be described either as renaissances, which re-discover and revitalize forgotten arts and values, or as revolutions, which break traditional bonds to initiate new arts and achieve new objectives. Most of the cultures of Western Europe have an easily recognized revolution in their history, but one Renaissance has usurped a central place among the renaissances and has acquired a capital *R*. The reawakening of the Renaissance, whatever its strands and whatever the period of its occurrence, profoundly affected culture for centuries. Yet no facts mark un-ambiguously the transition from the Middle Ages to the Renaissance, and no characteristics in any of the strands of human activity, art, or thought are found in the one and not in the other period. Therefore after centuries of dogmatism, reinforced by the mounting data of research and criticism about the achievements and innovations of the Renaissance, we have moved, after the manner of the history of culture, into a century of increasing pluralism and skepticism in the interpretation of the Renaissance.

The facts about the Renaissance are facts about the arts — the fine arts, the practical arts, the theoretic arts, and the liberal arts by which the arts are interpreted, understood, and given their form and characteristics. The liberal arts are practiced in writing the history of culture, and the differences between nineteenth and twentieth-century histories and analyses of the Renaissance are due in part to differences in the facts uncovered, alleged, credited, and interpreted, and in part to differences in the historical and liberal arts which orient research and re-construction to the observation, elaboration, establish-ment, and construction of different relevant facts. The history of the liberal arts is, therefore, not only a central

159

part of the history of the Middle Ages and the Renaissance, but a unique instrument to provide an objective basis for distinctions which must remain relative and subjective unless the cultural framework and commitment of the historian is taken into account in considering the facts and interpretations from which he constructs the Renaissance. Many of the changes which occurred in the fourteenth century were noticed and elaborated in the fifteenth and sixteenth centuries and reached unmistakably clear developments in the seventeenth and eighteenth centuries. If the eighteenth century is taken as the point of triangulation, changes may be detected in the early Renaissance which mark different emphases, meanings, and directions in the complex movements of thought and expression in Western Europe from the Roman Empire to the late fourteenth century which distinguish the entire period from the characteristic developments from the early Renaissance to the late eighteenth century. The uses of the liberal arts suggest four strands in which those changes in the liberal arts may be detected: (1) the conception and development of the liberal arts themselves as disciplines and as subject matters, (2) the organization of the liberal arts as knowledge of things and of words, as programs of education and learning, and as encyclopedias of knowledge and of facts, (3) the authors or authority of the accomplishments of men worthy of analysis and interpretation, of biography and bibliography, by the liberal arts, and (4) the facts and occurrences that provide the circumstances, and the achievements of men in those circumstances, set forth by the liberal arts as history.

1. The Liberal Arts as Disciplines
and as Subject Matters

If one projects back from the eighteenth century to the fourteenth century, it is clear that important changes had occurred in the liberal arts. During the Middle Ages the liberal arts had been the seven arts of the trivium and the quadrivium — the arts of words: grammar, rhetoric, and logic or dialectic; and the arts of things: arithmetic, geometry, astronomy, and music. During the Middle Ages, it was clear, the verbal arts had predominated and among the arts of the trivium, logic had carried the field since, of course, Aristotle had enslaved men's minds for a thousand years. There had been a battle of the arts, between logic and rhetoric, in the thirteenth century, grammar had played a prominent place in the thought and education of the twelfth century, and the elements of mathematics and cosmology were available in twelfth-century translations from Arabic, but none of these departures from logical formalisms and abstraction was influential until the fourteenth century. The *Ars Magna* of Raymund Lully (ca. 1235-1315) was remembered and used by sixteenth and seventeenth-century philosophers; the reforms of Ramus and other sixteenth-century philosophers and critics, which transformed the traditional liberal arts of words and of mathematics, had earlier beginnings; the arts of things had begun to emerge in the mechanical and physical arts, from the complex developments of the arts of mathematics and logic, and had come to full development in the seventeenth century; the new liberal arts of literature or philology and of history had begun to take shape; and philosophy had been freed from the domina-

161

tion of theology to contemplate the world of art and of science.

Viewed from the vantage point of the twentieth century and of changed conceptions of the arts and sciences, the facts on which this characterization of the Renaissance (which was developed from views which the Renaissance humanists expressed about medieval arts and misconceptions from which they were awakened) are dubious or false. More important, however, even if they were corrected and supplemented with other like facts, they are not the facts which are relevant or critical to understanding the liberal arts of the Middle Ages and the Renaissance. The liberal arts were invented and developed by the Greeks; they were enumerated, systematized, and organized by the Romans. The Romans called them the "liberal" arts, the "human" arts, the "good" arts. They were the arts of free men and "more human" men, since *humanitas* is apparent in the accomplishments of great men, and all learning or knowledge forms a "cycle" of interdependent arts, an *enkuklios paideia* or *encyclopaedia*, both in programs of education and in organizations of knowledge and compendiums of facts. The medieval version of the liberal arts was based on the Roman formulation, particularly as it was elaborated by Cicero, with rectifications borrowed from the Platonic or Neoplatonic tradition to adapt the pagan arts to a Christian God, a Christian cosmos, and a Christian history. The Renaissance version of the liberal arts based its correction of errors in the medieval version on Cicero improved with Neoplatonic adaptations. The two versions are therefore comparable and distinguishable in their statements of the arts as disciplines, as organized in encyclopedias, as bearing on the authors of humane ac-

162

complishments, and as discernible in the concrete facts and values of history.

Medieval conceptions of the liberal arts were derived from Cicero (particularly the *De Inventione* and the Ciceronian *Ad Herennium*), Martianus Capella, Apuleius, and Macrobius. According to Cicero, the study of eloquence had been disjoined from the study of wisdom after Socrates. The ideal for rhetoric and philosophy was to rejoin them. An art of discourse (*ratio disserendi*) consists of two parts, invention or discovery and judgment or proof. In the *Marriage of Philology and Mercury*, Martianus Capella presents the joining of Mercury, or eloquence, to philology, or the love of theory or reason, with the seven liberal arts acting as verbose, didactic bridesmaids. Augustine adapted Plato's analysis of physics, logic, and ethics, as the three parts of philosophy, to the triune God of Christian theology, and put the liberal arts to hermeneutic uses in interpreting the texts of scripture and the facts of history and of the cosmos, and to demonstrative and persuasive uses in ordering Christian doctrine and in extending Christian truths. What little was known of Aristotle during the Middle Ages was fitted into this project. All that was known was Boethius's translation of two books of Aristotle's logic, the *Categories* and *On Interpretation* (Boethius wrote that he had also translated the *Prior Analytics*, and many medieval manuscripts of his translations contain a version of that work, in two recensions which have been published in 1962; but if it is Boethius's translation, there is no evidence that it was read or had any influence prior to the twelfth century), and that little was colored by the Neoplatonic setting Boethius gave it: Boethius translated Porphyry's *Introduction* to the

Categories, which interprets categories in terms derived from the dialectical reasoning of the *Topics*, and Boethius's *On Topical Differences* taught the Middle Ages to treat the logic of the sciences as dialectical rather than apodictical proof.

During the early Middle Ages grammar was an art of interpretation as well as the art of speaking correctly; the study of literature was a branch of grammar in the twelfth century. Rhetoric was a hermeneutic art as well as the art of speaking well; it was used as the method of resolving the contradictions of conflicting formulations in the development of canon law and as the method of the interpretation of scripture and history. The fact that the third art of the trivium was sometimes called logic, sometimes dialectic, is due in part to the old opposition of Aristotelian logic to Platonic dialectic. They were merged in the early Middle Ages: the logical element lacks grounding in Aristotelian logical principles because the *Posterior Analytics* was untranslated, unreported, and unknown; the dialectical element owes more to Aristotle's formulation of dialectic in the *Topics* than to the dialectic Plato used in the dialogues, and that Aristotelian element was known by way of Cicero and Themistius whom Boethius mingled in his *On Topical Differences*. The last four books of Aristotle's *Organon* — the *Prior Analytics*, *Posterior Analytics*, *Topics*, and *On Sophistical Refutations* — were translated in the twelfth century, and came to be known as the *logica nova* in contrast to the *logica vetus*, the *Categories*, and *On Interpretation*. The *Posterior Analytics* had little influence in the twelfth century (John of Salisbury writes that although he had several courses on it, he knew no professor who understood it or used it in any science except mathematics[1]), and principles were still treated as dialectical probabilities or as sophisms, explored more fully with the aid of Aristotle's treatises. The *Posterior Analytics* was the subject of commentaries in the thirteenth and fourteenth centuries, but the logic based on apodictic principles was called the *logica antiqua* in contrast to the *logica moderna* based on dialectical or paradoxical principles, which was the logic taught in the schools in the form of analyses of the properties of terms and of dialectical and sophistical reasoning in the *summulae logicales* or in the form of dialectics of signifying, understanding, and being in the *speculative grammars*. The discussion of the quadrivium in the early Middle Ages was based on Boethius's treatises *De Institutione Arithmetica* and *De Institutione Musica*, and on the treatise *Geometria* attributed to him, plus some devices of Arabic notation added by Gerbert in the tenth century. Translations from the Arabic in the twelfth and thirteenth centuries added perspective or optics, and algebra to the arts of the quadrivium, and the logical treatises on the hypothetico-deductive inferences of dialectic (as contrasted to the categorico-deductive inferences of logic) and the applications of hypothetical dialectic and sophisms to mathematics and kinetics laid methodological bases for later advances in mathematics and physics.

Renaissance criticisms of the verbalism, logic chopping, and irrelevant abstractness of the medieval liberal arts were reactions against the developments of the fourteenth century. These judgments were honored and repeated in historical characterizations of the Middle Ages until, from the vantage point of nineteenth- and twentieth-century advances in mathematical logic and philosophical grammar, we have begun to understand, appreciate, and use fourteenth-century theories. The criticism of the arts was reinforced by substantive criticism of the consequent failure of philosophers and theologians trained in those arts to appreciate the rhetoric and the meanings of ancient philosophers and church fathers.

Grammar became regulative and normative grammar; and the exegetical function was taken over, and transformed from an interpretation of content to an interpretation of text, by a new liberal art, philology or literature or criticism. When Guillaum Budé published his treatise *On Philology* in 1530, philology had become the art of editing, emending, and studying texts rather than the love of knowledge whose marriage to eloquence had been facilitated by the liberal arts as bridesmaids.

Rhetoric had become an art of persuasion, with a dialectical form and a subject matter derived from the classics of literature and oratory; and the function of interpreting concrete facts had been taken over and transformed from a rhetoric of debate to a rhetoric of factual and consequential narration in the new liberal art of history. Rudolph Agricola transformed the methods of Cicero's *De Inventione* in his *De Inventione Dialectica* in 1480, and when Ramus reviewed the errors of Quintilian, Cicero, and Aristotle in the sixteenth century (Quintilian's errors exceeded those of Cicero and Aristotle, and Cicero's those of Aristotle), he rectified them by analyzing the use of metaphors, causes, topics, and syllogisms in the works of orators and poets. Bodin defined history as true narration in his *Method for the Easy Understanding of History* in 1622.

Logic became constructive or divisive dialectic in the *summulae logicales* and in Ramus, and "etymological" and "diasynthetic" grammar in the speculative grammars; and the function of establishing principles was taken over and transformed by a new liberal art, philosophy or method. The last three books of Aristotle's *Organon* treated demonstrative or apodictic, dialectical or probabilistic, and sophistical or paradoxical principles; during the Renaissance logical works substituted for such principles a treatise on *method*, in the large sense develped in Giacomo Aconcio's *On Method, that is, on the Right Reason of Investigating and Treating the Arts and Sciences* (1558), and that reduction was canonized in modern "Aristotelian" logic by the influence of the Port Royal *Logic* (1662) in which three books concerned with subject matter treated in the first three books of Aristotle's *Organon* are followed by a fourth and final book on *Method*.[2]

The renaissance of the quadrivium, or the sciences of things, in the sixteenth and seventeenth centuries laid the beginnings of the modern development of physics and mathematics and explored the relations between the two, sometimes reducing mathematics to the mechanical art of measurement, sometimes making physics a part of the universal science of mathematics; and in the process science became one of the liberal arts to prepare the way for liberal arts colleges which became colleges of arts and sciences as place was found for the sciences in the curriculum of studies.

Conceptions of the liberal arts were highly diversified during the Middle Ages and the Renaissance, and opposed theories of each of the arts were developed in each period which often continued, in later theories and applications, words and distinctions developed and used earlier. Yet from the vantage point of the twentieth century it is possible to discern common characteristics in medieval theories of the liberal arts which were changed radically in the early Renaissance and to trace the development of new characteristics from the Renaissance to the eighteenth century in modern conceptions and theories of the liberal arts. The medieval liberal arts were universal *disciplines*, each of them applicable to any subject matter; the Renaissance liberal arts were particular *subject matters*, which could be explored anew by taking up where classical statements and examples of them left off and which were each potentially universal in scope. The medieval liberal arts were grammar, rhetoric, logic or dialectic, arithmetic, geometry, astronomy, and music. Viewed as subject matters they were limited and incomplete, unless many other arts were added to them, but they could be unified in the new liberal arts of beautiful letters or *belles lettres* and beautiful arts or *beaux arts*, in history or true narration, in science or the laws of motion and change, in philosophy or method, and in social science or the structure of associated behavior, and each of the new arts could be made inclusive and architectonic of all activities and all arts. The transformation of the liberal arts in the early Renaissance was a reaction and response to the degradations or inadequacies of arts conceived as disciplines: they tend to become universal, abstract, verbal, and to lose connection with the particularities of circumstances, subject matters, and problems. The transformation in the nineteenth and twentieth centuries of the liberal arts which were developed from beginnings made in the Renaissance is a reaction and response to the degradations and inadequacies of arts conceived as subject matters: they tend to become fragmented, to multiply, and to lose connection with each other and with the common problems and matters of daily life from which they selected aspects for precise methodological analysis. We are still engaged in working out the implications of that reaction, and one manifestation of the response has been the suspicion of nineteenth-century characterizations of the Renaissance based on conceptions formed in the Renaissance, without rectification in the light of current conceptions of the liberal arts.

2. The Liberal Arts as Programs of Education and as Encyclopedias of Knowledge and of Facts

Roman philosophers and educators had organized knowledge and learning in a cycle or circle of interdependent arts, an *enkuklios paideia* or *encyclopaedia*. Programs of education and compendiums of knowledge and information were encyclopedias. Cicero had defined wisdom as science or knowledge (*scientia*) of things human and divine; the liberal arts were the arts by which that knowledge was acquired and transmitted by men. Christian philosophers and theologians continued the definition of wisdom as the definition of philosophy, sometimes specifying that it is *probable* knowledge, such as is possible to man, of things divine and human, and further specifying that philosophy is the art of arts and the discipline of disciplines. The liberal arts were disciplines, not subject matters, and philosophy was the discipline of the discipline of all knowledge and action. Augustine had applied the liberal arts to the organization of Christian doctrine and education: when he wrote the *De Doctrina Christiana*, he knew, as we tend to forget, that *doctrina* means both teaching and what is taught. Boethius expounded the liberal arts, not logic alone, and applied them explicitly to theology in his theological treatises. The early medieval "encyclopedists" organized the cycle of the arts during the sixth and seventh centuries, and since the liberal arts were arts of words and things, they wrote encyclopedias which presented both kinds of knowledge whether it was a compendium of language or of nature.

Cassiodorus's *Institutions of Divine and Secular Letters* is a small encylcopedia of arts; and Cassiodorus knew, as we tend to forget, that *institutio* means both arrangement and instruction — he might also have known that it means custom and he might have anticipated that it means institution. The *Institutions* is in two books, the first concerned with the Old and New Testaments, the second with the seven liberal arts. The *Etymologies* (also called *Origins*) of Isidore of Seville analyzes the nature of all things, in twenty books, by examining the words applied to them. The seven liberal arts are treated in the first three books, medicine in Book 4, law and chronology in Book 5, and ecclesiastical books and offices in Book 6. The last fourteen books proceed according to subject matter from God, angels, and the faithful (Book 7), through the Church (Book 8), languages and society (Book 9), man, animals (Books 10-12), geography (Books 13-14), and the practical arts (Books 15-20), ending with food and drink, and domestic and rural implements (Book 20). Book 10 is a dictionary of Latin words arranged alphabetically (Isidore did not realize, as we do, that the alphabetical arrangement of encyclopedias was invented after Gutenberg, and is part of the complex imposed on men's minds by the invention of printing). Isidore wrote a great variety of encyclopedias, among others *On the Nature of Things*, which covers meteorology and astronomy; *Differences and Properties of Words* in two books, one on the differences of words, the other on the differences of things; and *On Illustrious Men*, a biographical encyclopedia. The Venerable Bede borrowed from and supplemented Isidore's work in his *On the Nature of Things*, as did Hrabanus Maurus in his *On the Universe*, which was also called *On the Nature of Things*.

The twelfth century saw a rebirth of the liberal arts and a recrudescence of encyclopedias. The *Heptateuchon* of Thierry of Chartres is a comprehensive compilation of long extracts from a great variety of sources on the seven arts; his *On the Works of the Six Days* employs the arts of the quadrivium on materials from *Genesis* and the *Timaeus*; he encouraged study and translation of works of Arabic science. Hugh of Saint Victor's *Didascalion* treats not only the seven liberal arts but also the seven mechanical arts (weaving, armory, navigation, agriculture, hunting, medicine, and theater), the parts of philosophy, and the parts of magic. Honorius of Autun wrote an encyclopedia *On the Image of the World* as well as *On Illustrious Men*. William of Conches made a compilation *On the Philosophy of the World* and Alexander Neckham on the *Natures of Things*. In the thirteenth century Thomas of Cantimpre wrote *On the Nature of Things* and Bartholomaeus Anglicus *On the Properties of Things*. Thomas arranges things in the sequence man, animals, plants, waters, stones and metals, astronomy and the elements; Bartholomaeus follows the sequence from God through angels, psychology, physiology, domestic economy, medicine, cosmology, chronology, birds, fishes, geography, minerals, trees, and animals to a final book on colors, odors, food, drink, weights, and measures. The *Summas* were encyclopedias of theology and philosophy, developed from the twelfth-century *Book of Sentences*, which ranged from God through the creation and the powers and actions, virtues and sins, institutions and sacraments of men to the last things; they were courses of instruction and compilations of doctrine. The *Summulae* were textbooks and encyclopedias of logic, ranging from the properties of terms to their composition in statements and arguments.

The medieval encyclopedias were organizations of disciplines as arts. It is difficult to separate the programs of education from the compilations of learning, and even the differences between words and things are related because both are known and set forth only by arts. The Renaissance encyclopedias were organizations of disciplines as subject matters. The beginnings of the transition to the Renaissance conception of the liberal arts are found in an increasingly sharp separation of programs of education from compendia, or ready reference books, of knowledge or information, both of which were called encyclopedias. The development of Renaissance programs of education led to the substitution of modern erudition for medieval wisdom and came to its culmination in nineteenth-century analyses of the methodology of *Naturwissenschaften* and *Geisteswissenschaften*, in which Dilthey made the culture and the arts of the Renaissance the crucial subject matter in the determination of the arts of humanistic or historical or cultural knowledge. The development of Renaissance compilations of knowledge led to the separation of dictionaries of things from dictionaries of words and to a competition among rival ways of classifying things according to history, biography, the mechanical arts, or the arts and sciences, which came to its culmination in nineteenth-century encyclopedic reactions to the French *Encyclopédie* of the eighteenth century.

Criticism of medieval methods of education during the early Renaissance took positive form in an endless series of treatises *De Ratione Studii* in the sixteenth century. Two of them, by Erasmus and Joachim Fortius Ringelbergius, were published together repeatedly, and a collection of Ringelberg's essays on teaching different subjects was published under the title *Lucubrationes vel potius Absolutissima* κυκλοπαιδεια in 1529. Antonio Possevino's *Selected Library [Bibliotheca] on the Organization of Studies [de Ratione Studiorum] in History, in the Disciplines, and in Procuring the Salvation of All* appeared in two folio volumes and eighteen books in 1593. The Jesuit *De Ratione Studiorum* was completed in 1599. A collection of twenty-four such treatises was published under the name of Grotius and others and with the little *De Studiis Instituendis* in 1645, and another collection under the name of Vossius with the title *De Studiis bene Instituendis* in 1658.

The organization of knowledge in these programs of education presented problems of differentiating and schematizing the fields of knowledge, which led to vast and learned disputes concerning erudition, "polymathy," "pansophy," and "polyhistory." Johannes Wowerius argued in his *Tractatio de Polymathia* in 1604 that grammar is improperly called polymathy, because it consists only of the science of speaking well and interpreting the poets, whereas polymathy requires all the liberal arts, the *enkuklios paideia*. Polymathy has two parts: *doctrine*, which consists in the cultivation of the best arts and sciences, and *science*, which employs the arts of inquiry concerning things themselves, and which requires both inspection of things and acquaintance with the works of those who excel in doctrine and erudition. Grammar is divided into three kinds: technical or methodic, exegetic (which includes history and is properly called "philology"), and critical (which is the most noble part, and consists of two parts concerned respectively with judgment and with the emendation of texts). *Polymathia* is *enkuklios paideia* in the proper sense. Commenius thought that three universal books were necessary, a *Pansophia*, a *Panhistoria*, and a *Pandogmatica*. Morhof's *Polyhistor, Literarius, Philosophicus et Practicus* in 1688 identified polymathy with "encyclopedia" or the circle of interrelated and independent arts, and J. M. Gesner's *First Lines of Introduction to Universal Erudition, namely, Philology, History, and Philosophy* was published in 1774.

Polymathy was universal erudition, but universal erudition tended to use the methods of philology or history or philosophy, and the encyclopedias which set forth all knowledge were collections of information about literature and authors, or about historical occurrences and the accomplishments of men, or about the truths certified by philosophy and by the arts and sciences. Literature is universal since it includes knowledge of everything that has been written, and the arts of criticism and history of literature are the methods of universal erudition. The long and voluminous development of the art of criticism reached a kind of culmination in Jean Le Clerc's *Ars Critica* in three volumes in 1698; the art of criticism has three parts: (1) on emendation, (2) on the indications by which spurious places and writings are distinguished from genuine, and (3) on judgment of the style and character of

174

the writer. Le Clerc edited a voluminous, periodical, encyclopedic "reader's digest" for the learned world, *Bibliothèque universelle et historique* (1686-93, 26 duodecimo volumes), *Bibliothèque choisie* (1703-13, 28 volumes), and *Bibliothèque ancienne et moderne* (1714-30, 29 volumes), in which, as one example, John Locke's *Essay* first appeared in French translation and abridgment. He also edited and revised Moreri's *Great Historical, Geographical, and Poetical Dictionary*.

History likewise is universal since it includes knowledge of everything that has happened, including the writing and careers of authors. The history of literature became bibliography and critical edition of texts and analytical judgment of styles, and gradually assimilated and eliminated literary criticism as interpretation of contents and judgment of forms in programs of education organized by subject matter. In the nineteenth century Dilthey projected a critique of historical reason to supplement Kant's critique of pure reason and to provide the method for the study of values and the humanities.

Philosophy, finally, reasserted its claim to universality not on the ground that it is the art of arts but because it is the knowledge of knowledges. The philosophers of the seventeenth century borrowed the method of the sciences to analyze human understanding and morals, and Francis Bacon's organization of knowledge provided the schematism to analyze human understanding and morals for the French *Encyclopédie* in the next century. Kant's Copernican revolution at the end of the eighteenth century sought the foundations and subject matter of philosophy not in a theoretic science of being but in a critical analysis of understanding, and in that analysis provided grounds for universality in science, morals, literature, and history.

The early beginnings of the transition from medieval compilations of knowledge to Renaissance compilations of information about things can be seen in the thirteenth century when Vincent of Beauvais required four mirrors in his *Speculum Majus* constructed to reflect "all things of all times," a natural, a doctrinal, a moral, and a historical mirror, and Brunetto Latini wrote his *Treasure of Books*. In the fourteenth century Pierre Bersuire classified things on a moral basis in the *Moral Reduction of the Whole Bible* in thirty-four books, the *Moral Reduction of the Properties of Things* in fourteen books, and the *Dictionary* of 3,512 terms arranged alphabetically and expounded morally. In the fifteenth century Giorgio Valla compiled an encyclopedia *On Things to be Sought and Things to be Avoided*, in which things are divided into three kinds — mental, bodily, and external. In the sixteenth century Gregory Reisch used two classifications, one according to the arts, the other according to subject matter in his *Margarita Philosophica*, and Raphael Maffei published his *Commentarii Urbani* in three tomes: "Geography," "Anthropology," and "Philology," and in that division "Philology" consists in a survey of knowledge according to subject matter, including the subject matter of the "cyclic" sciences.

In the evolution from the Renaissance to the eighteenth century, dictionaries and lexicons were expanded to include terms from the arts and sciences, and then two kinds of dictionaries were distinguished, dictionaries of words and dictionaries of things. Early encyclopedias were often called dictionaries of arts, science, and eventually of trades and handicrafts (*métiers*). One of the problems treated in the prefaces and in the bodies of these works was how to relate the technical terms compiled in alphabetical order to the arts and sciences of which they were parts. The vocabularies or lexicons of Totellius, Junianus Maius, Reuchlin, and Dionysius Novariensis had appeared in the fifteenth century before the Latin dictionary of Calepinus, published in 1502, became so influential that the term "calepin" became a common noun. Robert Estienne published the *Thesaurus Linguae Latinae*, a reprint of Calepinus, in 1532, and subsequently enlarged it. Henri Estienne published the *Thesaurus Graecae Linguae* in five folio volumes in 1572, and his assistant Scapula published an unauthorized one-volume abridgment in 1579. Hadrian Junius published a Greek-Latin Lexicon and an *Octolingual Nomenclator, containing the Proper Names of all Things*. Commenius published several Gateways of Languages. The word "dictionary" was used in the title of Charles Estienne's *Dictionarium Historicum ac Poëticum* in 1553, which was translated and expanded in Juigné-Broissinière's *Dictionnaire Théologique, Géographique, Poétique, Cosmographique, et Chronologique*.

The dictionary of the Italian language, published by the Accademia della Crusca in 1612, was designed to define and purify a living language, as was the dictionary of the French language on which the French Academy started work in 1639. The design of both was to exclude words belonging specifically to the arts and sciences. Abbè Antoine Furetière was expelled from the French Academy for planning another dictionary giving all the terms of the sciences and the arts. In 1680 César Pierre Richelet's dictionary included terms of history, grammar, criticism, jurisprudence, and other arts. Furetière's *Universal Dictionary, containing generally all French Words, Old as well as*

Modern, and the Terms of all the Sciences and the Arts was issued in three volumes in 1690. The French Academy responded by commissioning Thomas Corneille, the brother of the playwright, to prepare *The Dictionary of Arts and Sciences* (the rivalry was carried even to the inversion of Sciences and Arts), which appeared in two volumes in 1694, the year in which the work on the dictionary of the French language was completed. Corneille also published a *Universal Geographic and Historical Dictionary* in 1708.

The encyclopedias of the seventeenth and eighteenth centuries took their diverse forms and plans from this separation and opposition of dictionaries of things from and to dictionaries of words. Some were biographical dictionaries; some were historical dictionaries; some were universal dictionaries of arts and sciences; some were technical encyclopedias. Moreri's *Le Grand Dictionnaire Historique, ou le Mélange Curieux de l'Histoire Sacrée et Profane* (1674) was reedited by Jean Le Clerc and was translated into English by Jeremy Collier as *The Great Historical, Geographical, and Poetical Dictionary*. Hofmann's *Lexicon Universale Historico-Geographico-Chronologico-Poëtico-Philologicum* (1677) is a dictionary of proper names of persons and places, and Bayle's *Dictionnaire Historique et Critique* (1697), which was to have included "real" as well as "personal" definitions, dropped in later editions the only two definitions of things which made their way into the first edition. The first alphabetical encyclopedia in English, John Harris's *Lexicon Technicum, or an Universal English Dictionary of Arts and Sciences* (1704), professes to explain not only the terms of art but the arts themselves. Harris's *Lexicon*, like Chauvin's *Lexicon Rationale sive Thesaurus Philosophicus* (1692) and Ephraim Chambers's *Cyclopaedia*,

178

or an Universal Dictionary of Arts and Sciences, containing an Explication of the Terms, and an Account of the Things Signified thereby, in the several Arts, both Liberal and Mechanical, and the several Sciences, Human and Divine . . . the Whole Intended as a Course of Ancient and Modern Learning (1728), included biographies and articles on geographical names.

The *Encyclopédie, ou Dictionnaire Raisonné des Sciences, des Arts et des Métiers* (1751-66), which was first planned as a translation and adaptation of Chambers's *Cyclopaedia*, has no articles on proper names, except those of emperors and other political rulers (that is, "historical" names); it has articles on schools of thought named after philosophers but no articles on the philosophers (that is, "philosophical" names), for example, an article on Epicureanism but none on Epicurus. The oppositions which set the *Universal Dictaryion of Furetière*, and the *Universal Dictionary of Trévoux* which was based on it, in controversial opposition to the *Dictionary* of the French Academy and the *Encyclopédie* were analyzed in detail in the prefaces to those dictionaries and in d'Alembert's "Preliminary Discourse." They were differences about things and words, and about the philosophic bases of organizations of knowledge and learning. D'Alembert explained the two parts of the title of the *Encyclopédie*: it was to be an "encyclopedia (*encyclopédie*)," that is, it was to expound the "order and concatenation of the parts of human knowledge," and it was to be an "analytical dictionary (*dictionnaire raisonné*) of the sciences, arts, and trades," that is, it was to set forth "for each science and for each art, liberal or mechanical, the general principles which are its basis and the most essential details which are its body and substance."[3] The order and parts adopted in the *Encyclopédie* are based on the organization of knowledge in the philosophy of Francis Bacon.

3. The Liberal Arts as Lives and Accomplishments of Men, the Humanities as Biography and Bibliography

The liberal arts in Rome were a cycle of interconnected disciplines which exhibited the accomplishments of man or humanity. In the Middle Ages, humanity was studied in human letters, and in the Renaissance humanity became plural in the humanities — literature, the fine arts, history, and philosophy. The encyclopedia, since it recorded and presented the accomplishments of great men, took its base in biography as well as in literature, history, and philosophy. The Dictionaries of the Renaissance had counterparts in the Libraries or *Bibliothecae*.

The medieval tradition of biography was established by the 135 lives in Jerome's *De Viris Illustribus* in 392. Jerome also calls them, in a letter, *De Scriptoribus Ecclesiasticis*. Suetonius had used the title, *On Illustrious Men*, for a collection of lives of men who had practiced the arts — the lives of poets, historians, philosophers, rhetoricians (or orators), and grammarians (or scholars). Jerome's writers were the Christian counterparts of such illustrious pagans. During the nine hundred years after Jerome, six writers added to the biographies of illustrious men or ecclesiastical writers: Gennadius of Marseilles in the fifth century, Isidore of Seville and Ildefonsus of Toledo in the seventh century, Sigebert of Gembloux in the eleventh century, Honorius of Autun in the twelfth century, and Henry of Ghent in the thirteenth century. The seven collections of lives were published in a single volume during and after the Renaissance — in 1580 by Suffridus Petrus under the composite title *De Illustribus Ecclesiae Scriptoribus*, in 1638 by Aubert Le Mire, under the title *Ecclesiastical Library or the Seven Ancient Nomenclators*, and in 1718 by J.A. Fabricius under the title *Bibliotheca Ecclesiastica*. Renaissance notes, additions, and commentaries were added. Erasmus was among the commentators on Jerome's *Lives*.

The study of ecclesiastical writers in the Renaissance was a first step toward the formation of the systematic bibliography of the eighteenth century. It was a transformation of brief lives of writers to lengthy specifications of titles and sketches of contents of works and circumstances of writers. John Tritheim's *Liber de Scriptoribus Eccelsiasticis* was published in 1494. Like Jerome, Tritheim includes non-Christian and nonecclesiastical writers (the younger Seneca, Philo Judaeus, and Josephus are in both collections), but Tritheim in his treatment of the fourteenth and fifteenth centuries finds it necessary to cross the line separating ecclesiastical writers from humanistic, scholarly, and lay authorities. The Libraries or *Bibliothecae* of ecclesiastical writers of the seventeenth century, from Robert Bellarmine through Philip Labbé, Casimir Oudin, Antonio Possevino, William Cave, and Louis Ellies du Pin worked and refined classifications of writers, oppositions of doctrines, tabulations of subjects covered. The materials requiring treatment were expanded so considerably that the third edition of du Pin's *New Library of Ecclesiastical Authors* (1693-1711) filled nineteen quarto volumes. Collections of *Bibliothecae*, in folio volumes, stand on library shelves next to similar folio volumes of ecclesiastical collections of "Annals," "Controversies," and "Judgments." The word "controversy" received its technical meanings in analyses of the arts and the contents of controversy, such as Bellarmine's *De Controversiis Christianae Fidei*, and the controversies of ecclesiastical writers led to the formation and opposition of religions and churches.

Libraries or *Bibliothecae* were compiled for all groupings of ecclesiastical writers. They were extended to writers who treat subjects relevant to religious questions, and finally to writers on all subjects grouped according to nationality or subject matter. They were compiled for the writers of the new religions; they had already been compiled for the writers who belonged to the old and the new religious orders; national collections of writers, ecclesiastical and nonecclesiastical, were compiled for the old and new nations; and the titles of the works of non-ecclesiastical writers were set forth and their contributions and positions were expounded in inclusive collections or libraries, and in collections specialized to particular subject matters. Tritheim, who wrote the first modern collection *On ecclesiastical writers*, also published collections *On the Luminaries of Germany*, *On Illustrious Benedictines*, and *A History of Illustrious Carmelites*. The character and limits of the transformation are exposed symbolically in the title of Jacob Gadd's *On Non-ecclesiastical Writers, Greek, Latin, and Italian, of the first Rank in the five Theaters, that is, Philosophical, Poetic, Historical, Oratorical, and Critical*, published in 1648-49. It includes many writers who are also treated in Libraries of Ecclesiastical Writers.

The sixteenth- and seventeenth-century Libraries and Collections and Indexes of illustrious writers of nations (German, Belgian, Dutch, Frisian, British, Irish, Scottish, Spanish) and of cities (Florence, Venice), which include the distinguished work of Pistorius, Foppens, Bale, Tanner, Leland, Pits, and many others, are still useful handbooks today. The Libraries or Lives of writers in the different fields of knowledge — medicine, law, history, philosophy, theology, literature and philology, science and various of the sciences — laid the foundations and assembled the data of the different fields which constituted the arts and sciences when they became subject matters rather than disciplines. In the process of the transformation, disciplines in turn were defined by, and identified with, subject matters. The overall collections of Libraries reached their comprehensive climax in the work of J. A. Fabricius, who edited in the late seventeenth and early eighteenth centuries a *Bibliotheca Ecclesiastica*, a *Bibliotheca Latina* in three volumes, a *Bibliotheca Graeca* (which grew from an original two to twelve quarto volumes), and a *Bibliotheca Latina Mediae et Infimae Aetatis*, in six volumes, which enshrines the transition from the Middle Ages in its title.

Medieval lives of writers or of illustrious men were short biographies designed to provide minimum information concerning authors widely read or encountered frequently in references or quotations. Renaissance Libraries of writers were bio-bibliographical compilations designed to provide comprehensive and specific information concerning books, recensions, and editions, positions and their interrelations, doctrines or methods and their respective authors or comparative ''authority,'' genres and periods of writings and their styles. Projection backward of the movements which resulted in the beginnings of systematic bibliography in the eighteenth century pinpoints the beginnings of those movements in the transition, during the early Renaissance, from liberal arts treated as universal disciplines applicable to any text or experience and used to distinguish and form particular subject matters from texts and experiences, to liberal arts treated as methods particular to the subject matters of literature, history, science, and philosophy, and each capable of universalization in organizing and ordering the subject matters of all arts and sciences. The medieval liberal arts were arts of interpretation and use of words and symbols applied to any subject matter. The Renaissance liberal arts were disciplines defined by fields and proper to subject matters. The meanings of words and symbols were determined and developed within the disciplines or subject matter fields, and dictionaries of things were compiled to supplement dictionaries of words. The investigation of *usages* proper to the dictionaries of words was separated from the investigation of *uses* proper to the dictionaries of things and of arts and science. They were distinct investigations because they had to do with different subject matters or disciplines, words and things.

Medieval "disputation" concerning the truth of a philosophical, theological, or scientific conclusion gave way to Renaissance "controversy" concerning the acceptability and applicability of opposed positions and methods in literature and the arts, fine and liberal; in biography and history, literary and political; in philosophy and method, scientific and humanistic; in religion and theology, natural and revealed. Biographical knowledge of the life of an author might be useful in the interpretation of his writings for the resolution of disputed questions, whereas information concerning the connections, derivations, and doctrinal foundations of an author might be useful for placing his position among those to be accepted, rejected, or modified. The authority of ecclesiastical authors depended, in the medieval use of the liberal arts, on their arguments, to be weighed in disputation and to be subject to deliberations of ecclesiastical authorities when the arguments touched questions of faith. The authority of authors depended, in the Renaissance use of the liberal arts, on positing and defending theses and positions and, in the case of adverse judgment of established authorities on matters of religious faith, on transference to, or establishment of, other ecclesiastical authorities or other nonecclesiastical jurisdictions. The authority of non-ecclesiastical writers, in like fashion, passed from deliberation in disputation, or calculating, or weighing (*disputatio*) of the contents of his works by use of the liberal arts, to judgment in controversy or turning against (*controversia*) the assumptions or methods of works when they are shown to depart from those of accepted authors, to battles of books, of ancients and moderns, in which values were sought in a rebirth of ancient arts and forms or in an innovation of new modes of expression and realization. The battles of books took place in libraries: the battle of the ancients and the moderns in literature, philosophy, and science, which was recorded by Swift in the eighteenth century, took place in Saint James Library; the battles of the nineteenth century of science and religion, initiated by Darwin and recorded by T. H. Huxley and Andrew D.White, and of spiritual psychology and empirical and experimental psychology, initiated by Wundt and Brentano, moved from libraries of books already written to fields of theory and observation; the battles of the twentieth century of philosophy and metaphysics, of psychology and physiology, of psychotherapy and medicine, and the recrudescence of the nineteenth-century battle of the two cultures, of the sciences and the humanities, moved to the libraries of departmental and disciplinary specialization to agitate, in the name of one of the disciplines and of one position concerning that discipline, for the institution of a new interdisciplinary Library by use of new conceptions and new media of communication.

For purposes of disputation, deliberation, and verification of arguments and consequences, theoretic and practical, a single volume could contain all the relevant information about the short list of illustrious men of a thousand years. For purposes of controversy, judgment, and justification of positions and conclusions, scientific, artistic, and technical, the lists of illustrious writers, nonecclesiastical as well as ecclesiastical, the enumeration of the titles of their works and the interpretation of their authenticity and intentions, in all nations and in all subject matters, lengthened and multiplied indefinitely for each century and each decade. It might easily seem to incautious interpreters and inattentive historians, who read titles but not works, that the transition from ecclesiastical to nonecclesiastical writers was a secularization of culture, that the multiplication of Libraries was a liberalization of judgment, and that the increase of authors and illustrious men was a sign of a new fecundity of invention and thought, as a result of which an astonishing percentage of the liberal artists of all time lived and worked in the Renaissance, much as an equally amazing percentage of scientists of all time live and work in the twentieth century. Such judgments, for all their plausibility and attractiveness, can be made safely and objectively only by conscious and careful use of the liberal arts, not only to certify and interpret "facts" but also to present and test criteria by which facts are "made" and interrelated, and data are "given" and constructed into facts.

4. The Liberal Arts as Concrete Values and Occurrences and Cultural Structures and Hierarchies of History

The history of the liberal arts in Rome was closely associated with the characterization and development of Roman culture and traditions. Cato the Elder, who opposed the study of Greek arts and literature because he feared that native Roman virtues might be sapped by effete foreign learning, wrote seven books of *Origins* on Roman history from the founding of Rome, and an encyclopedic handbook for his son on morals, sanitation, oratory, military science, agriculture, and other subjects. Varro, one of the great encyclopedists, wrote forty-one books of *Antiquities of Things Human and Divine* (which is referred to frequently in Augustine's *On the City of God against the Pagans*), fifteen books of *Imagines*, containing biographies and portraits of 700 famous Greeks and Romans, and nine books of *Disciplines*, in which medicine and architecture, and the seven arts which became the medieval liberal arts, are treated. Cicero judges Roman literature deficient in history, which is closer than any other branch of literature to rhetoric; he makes this judgment in *The Laws*, one of the works he composed, in his enforced leisure from politics, to make philosophy and Greek philosophy available to his countrymen. Roman historians continued to write the history of Rome from the foundation of the city, but as the empire grew and *ius civile* was supplemented by *ius gentium,* the history of Rome became the history of the world, with supplementary accounts of barbarian peoples conquered by the empire or bounding the empire; and it could be divided into periods by the lives of the Caesars, supplemented by the lives of other illustrious men.

The development of the liberal arts in Christian thought was likewise closely associated with the development and characterization of the culture and cult of Christians. The antiquities of divine and human things were to be found in the Old Testament, and the adjustment of Jewish history to pagan history presented serious problems of simultaneity and sequence, of synchrony and diachrony. The Alexandrian chronologists had used the Trojan war and the Olympiads as beginning points and periods for their chronology. Eusebius of Caesaria (ca. 265-340) used the year of Abraham at the beginning of the canon and three columns of dates at the end: the Olympiad, the year after Christ, and the year of the Roman Emperor. In this fashion a series of nine synchronic dates is provided for the institution of the laws of Lycurgus — eleven hundred and ninety sixth year of Abraham and a place in the columns of kings of Judaea, Israel, Assyria, Corinth, Lacedaemonia, Athens, the Latins, and the Egyptians — and Abraham is synchronized with Ninus, Moses with Cecrops, Samson with the Trojan War. Eusebius also wrote an *Ecclesiastical Histories.* Jerome translated Eusebius's *Chronicle* into Latin, adapted it, and extended it from the year A.D. 325 to 378 (Jerome's *Chronicle* is our *only* historical source of information about the life of Lucretius). In addition to providing a schematism of synchrony and diachrony, Eusebius laid the foundations of periodization. In Jerome's version of Eusebius's *Chronicle* there are five ages: (1) Abraham (b. 2016-5 B.C.) to the Trojan war, (2) to the first Olympiad, (3) to the second year of the reign of Darius, (4) to the death of Christ, (5) to the twentieth year of the reign of Constantine. The antiquity of Moses is unmistakably established.

Augustine divided the history of the world into six ages, and Isidore of Seville popularized and extended that schematism. The six ages of the world, according to Augustine, corresponded to the six days of creation, for in the eyes of the Creator a thousand years is as a day, and the seventh day is the unending Sabbath of creation. The pagan historians of Rome had traced the long series of events which culminated in Imperial Rome on the analogy of the development of man; Florus, thus, in the preface to his *Epitome of Roman History*, distinguishes four ages — infancy, youth, maturity, and old age, to be followed, Florus hopes, by another period of youth — and medieval historians adapted that analogy. The Alexandrian chronologists also developed a cyclical periodization by the four empires of the world which was reformulated in the second century after Christ by Ptolemy. The four empires of the world were given a historical impetus and end in Christian historiography by Daniel's interpretation of the dream of Nebuchadnezzar in which he saw an image with head of gold, breast and arms of silver, belly and thighs of brass, legs of iron, and feet partly iron and partly clay; according to Daniel, these were four successive kingdoms, which will be followed, after the destruction of the kingdom of iron and clay, by a kingdom of

God which shall never be destroyed. The four empires were identified by Jerome in his commentary on the book of Daniel: the Assyrians and Babylonians, the Medes and the Persians, the Macedonians and the Diadochi, and the Romans which is destined to last, according to Jerome, to the end of the world. Pompeius Trogus, without the aid of Daniel, had treated them as five empires: Assyria, Media, Persia, Macedonia, and Rome. The four empires appear in Hippolytus, Origen, Eusebius, Jerome, and Augustine; they recur with their dynamic of successive destruction during the Middle Ages and the Renaissance; they appear in Renaissance histories, such as Sleidanus's *De Quattuor Summis Imperiis* with the German empires as the fourth empire, and the theory is rejected by Bodin in the sixteenth century because he finds more than four empires, and Toynbee in the twentieth century presents twenty-one empires with unchanged historic doom and with doubts about the twenty-second eternal empire of peace.

The tasks attributed to Roman and Christian historians were similar, but with inverse perspectives: the pagans traced the growth of Roman glory; the Christians separated the growth of the Christian religion from the decline of Roman power and glory; the pagans recorded the histories of barbarians conquered or on the periphery of the empire; the Christians wrote the histories of invaders and conquerors of the empire. Augustine wrote *On the City of God against the Pagans* to demonstrate that the glory of Rome had not depended on pagan religion, and Orosius worked out the details of the case in *Seven Books of Histories against the Pagans*. Cassiodorus wrote a *History of the Goths* and a *Chronicle* from Adam to the year 519. Gregory of Tours wrote a *History of the Franks* which begins with a brief compendium of world history. Isidore of Seville wrote a *Chronicle* from Creation to 616 divided into six ages, a *History of the Kings of the Goths, the Vandals, and the Suevi,* and a collection *On Illustrious Men.* The Venerable Bede wrote a *Chronicle or on the Six Ages of the World,* and an *Ecclesiastical History of the English People.* Paul the Deacon wrote a *History of the Langobard People,* a *Book of the Bishops of Metz,* and a *Historia Romana,* an amplified and extended version of Eutropius. From the twelfth century on, the almost innumerable series of chronicles may be divided into three general kinds: (1) those grouped about the personal experiences of an important actor in important events, such as the Crusades, (2) those which center about a single monastery, and (3) chronicles of towns.

At the end of the eleventh century Sigebert de Gembloux wrote a *Chronicle* which begins in 381, as a continuation of the *Chronicle* of Eusebius, and ends in 1112, the year of Sigebert's death. Further continuations were written by several authors. Sigebert also wrote a history of the *Deeds of the Abbots of Gembloux* and a *Book on Ecclesiastical Writers* (which contains a good bibliography of his own works). Honorius of Autun wrote a *Summa totius seu de omnimoda Historia,* of which only part has been published (although it exists complete in manuscript), the beginning and the end, starting with the year 726, and a collection of lives of illustrious men, *De Luminaribus Ecclesiae.* William of Malmesbury deals with English and modern history in *On the Deeds of the Kings of the English* and *Historia Novella.* Guibert of Nogent's *De Pignoribus Sanctorum* goes into historical questions of the authenticity of remains of

191

saints, and William of Newburgh's *History of English Things* contains reflections on history which have merited him the name of Father of Historical Criticism according to Freeman. Otto of Freising wrote a *Chronicle of History of the two Cities* from Adam to the year 1146 and a *Deeds of Emperor Frederick I.* The two cities are the earthly city of Babylon and the heavenly city of Jerusalem. Otto lists his sources in the *Prologus* to the Chronicle: Pompeius Trogus, Justin, Tacitus, Varro, Eusebius, Jerome, Orosius, Jordanes, and many others, but he says that he follows particularly Augustine and Orosius. He makes use of Trogus's conception of the conflict of freedom and power (*imperium*) and the transference of power (*translatio imperium*) from empire to empire in Jerome's version of the four empires, and he finds a place for the development of philosophy and logic in the *Chronicle* and for the debates about the liberal arts in the twelfth century in the *Deeds*.

Joachim of Floris and his followers divided world history into three ages, the first under the Father and governed by married people following the Old Testament, the second under the Son and governed by secular clergy following the New Testament, and the third under the Holy Spirit and governed by regular clergy following the Eternal Gospel. In the first, God manifested himself through the works of his eternal power and ruled by law and fear; in the second, Christ revealed himself through mysteries and ordinances of faith; and in the third, for which the others have been merely preparatory, the mind will see truth face to face without the veil of symbols; the heart will be filled with a love which excludes all selfishness and dread; and the will, freed from sin, will need no law over it but will be a law to itself. Joachimite views influenced Dante, Paracelsus, Postel, Campanella, Bodin, Bacon, Descartes, Pascal, and Lessing, and they have had a widespread renewal in the twentieth century.

In the thirteenth century Roger Bacon traced the varying fortunes of mankind, and the history of thought and science, from Adam by relating the inspiration of grace to the progress of experimental science and the degradations of vice to the causes of ignorance. The *Flowers of History* of Roger Wendover extends from the creation to the year 1234, and the *Greater Chronicle* of Matthew Paris continues the account to 1259. Matthew also wrote a *History of the English*.

As the biographies of ecclesiastical writers could be reduced to a short list of illustrious writers to which successive biographers added short lives of more recent illustrious writers, so the chronicles of the Middle Ages could recount the ages since Adam in a sequence to which later historians could add the events of recent decades. As the biographies changed to bio-bibliographies when the focus changed from universal disciplines to particular subject matters, and the subject matter was divided according to the nationality of the author and the field of his inquiry and work, with a consequent vast increase in the number of authors and works to be recorded in the numerous Libraries, so histories of periods and peoples and kings changed to accounts of happenings and actions and agents when the focus changed from the structure of historical change to the subject matter of concrete events and of actions of particular communities and men. Both the annals of particular monasteries, towns, and other communities, and the universal chronicles or histories from Adam to the present continued from the Middle Ages through the Renaissance; at most, citizens and statesmen who made use of documents and knowledge of affairs began to write annals, chronicles, and memoirs, and the last stages of universal histories began to reflect the claims, rhetorics, and policies of new religions and the old religion and the oppositions of new empires and old empires in power and glory. But history was not an art during the Middle Ages; it used all the arts and particularly, on the authority of Cicero, the art of rhetoric. The transformation of the arts during the early Renaissance prepared the way for the emergence in the fifteenth and sixteenth centuries of the arts of history and the methods of history as a stage to the development of a battle of opposition or amalgamation of scientific methods and historical methods which reached its climax in the nineteenth century.

The beginnings of the art of history may be discerned in Petrarch's sense of affinity with ancient authors, to whom he wrote a series of letters, and to their times, and in his consequent study of the manuscripts of Livy's history of Rome from its foundation to Livy's own times. This sense of an affinity with Roman writers and Roman eloquence and his distaste for Aristotelian dialectic and Averroistic disputes bodies forth the historical topography of a middle period of rhetorical insensitivity. Petrarch wrote a collection of *Things to be Remembered*, four books presenting the opinions of ancient writers and illustrious men and of recent thinkers (*recentiores*) on a series of topics, but none of the positions taken by thinkers during the middle period, and an *Epitome of Lives of Illustrious Men*, all ancient Romans, to which Lobardus wrote a supplement. The pupils and admirers of Petrarch gave history a prominent place in education and published the first edition of Livy, which seems to have owed much to Petrarch's paleographical studies. Vigerius gives history the first place among liberal studies, placing it before "moral philosophy" and "eloquence" in his *De Ingenuis Moribus*.[4] The growing enthusiasm for history and for the study of Livy laid the basis not only for the development of an art of history in contrast to the medieval rhetorical study of history but also for a battle of the books concerning the art of history, which began in the sixteenth century and continued to the nineteenth.

Rhetoric had special connections with, and applications to, history in the Middle Ages and in the Renaissance, which are reflected in the changing methods of rhetoric and nature of history. Medieval rhetoric provided the commonplaces by which to analyze and judge arguments concerning concrete occurrences and problems — whether they occurred, what they were, how they were qualified and connected, and how they should be judged. The use of rhetoric to constitute the art of history in the Renaissance resulted in two versions of history depending on two arts of rhetoric, a literary history using the devices of philology and a political history using the devices of politics and jurisprudence. Similar differences had separated demonstrative or epidictic rhetoric, which led to the literary style of the Second Sophistic, from legal rhetoric in Rome; and in legal rhetoric, in turn, judicial or forensic rhetoric was distinguished from deliberative or political rhetoric. These differences led in the Renaissance to a battle between humanists and lawyers, and to an echoing battle within jurisprudence between scholars who sought to edit the texts and study the history of ancient law and scholars who sought to apply the principles of the Roman jurisconsults and to extend the system of law. The battle concerning the true art or the most useful method of history — of writing, reading, teaching, studying, or understanding history — merged with the battle concerning the art and method of law — of natural, conventional, and statute law, of universal law and particular customs, of freedom and power, of virtue and honor, of *honestas* and *utilitas*, of administrative, legislative, and judicial powers — and with the battle concerning the art and method of literature — of the history of literature and the criticism of literature.

The humanistic study of history continued Petrarch's work of discovering and collating texts and manuscripts of the ancient historians, and turned to the consideration of questions of reading, teaching, appreciating, and using history. The historical arts and the teaching of history had secured some spread of acceptance when Machiavelli criticized the teaching of history in 1516-1517 in his *Discourses on Livy*. The example of antiquity is imitated in the fine arts, but ancient virtues and institutions are more admired than imitated. In the science of medicine the experience of ancient physicians is taken by their successors as a guide, and modern jurists might make similar use of the decisions of jurisconsults if their judgments were reduced to a system. This failure to use the examples of antiquity is due to a lack of real knowledge of history. Machiavelli was resolved to open a new route and use a new method to investigate how a republic is founded, governed, maintained, and extended.[5] The method turns out to be the method that Cicero had used in the *De Re Publica* — the examination, not of a perfect state imagined by a wise man in the manner of the Greeks, but of the history of Rome in which the wisdom of generations of men contributed to build an actual perfect state which was kept operative by the separation and balance of monarchical, aristocratic, and democratic powers in a mixed constitution.

The historical arts were even further developed in doctrine, and more definitely set in controversial oppositions, when Bodin published his *Methodus ad Facilem Historiarum Cognitionem* in 1566 and in an enlarged second edition in 1572. In his *Dedicatory Epistle* to Jean Tessier, the close connection between the methods of law, history, and literature becomes apparent, since laws and customs are the chief subject matter of history, if the interpretation of texts of all sorts can be saved from the pestilence of grammar which has afflicted all disciplines — philosophy, oratory, mathematics, and theology as well as jurisprudence. There are three entirely different ways of writing: (1) inventing subjects and developing them, (2) ordering matters and polishing forms, or (3) correction of old books. The first of these methods is practiced by the commentators of Roman law to such an extent that they do not know what their art is, for, Bodin reminds Tessier, arts and sciences are of universals, not of singulars.[6] Bodin argues that it is absurd to seek to establish universal law on Roman laws, and he proposes instead to study the laws of all peoples and to use the method of Plato to order them in a table of universal law and so to repair the damage done by the ancient commentators, who wrote in a period which had no place for the "good arts" and *"humanitas."* There are no fruits of history richer than those which are gathered concerning the state of Republics; the end of the method is to study public affairs or the appreciation of Laws.[7]

Bodin distinguishes three interrelated kinds of history — human, natural, and divine — before arguing that it is wise to begin with human history.

There are three kinds of history, that is, of true narration: human, natural, and divine. The first pertains to man, the second to nature, the third to the parent of nature. The first explicates the actions of man acting his life in society; the second deduces the causes posited in nature and their development from a first principle; the last perceives the force and power of the sovereign God and immortal spirits as they are in themselves. From these arise a threefold assent [*assentio*] — probable, necessary, and religious — and as many virtues, namely, prudence, science, and religion. The first separates the disgraceful [*turpe*] from the honorable or good [*honestum*], the second the true from the false, the third piety from impiety. The first derives its title as moderator of human life from the rule of reason and the use of things to be done; the second has its title as discoverer of all things from the investigation of hidden causes; the third has its title as expeller of vices from the love of one God for us. These three virtues conjoined to each other give rise to true wisdom, the supreme and final good of man: those who partake of this good in this life are called happy or blessed [*beati*].[8]

Like Machiavelli, Bodin opposed the philological or literary arts of history, and sought an historical method adapted to understanding public affairs or republics and principalities. Unlike Machiavelli, he did not seek the history of republics in the interpretation of Livy or the history of Rome but in the study of the laws of all peoples, and unlike the German historians he did not seek the evolution of republics in the transference of powers through four empires but in a table of universal law in which the divisions of law can be deduced from the principles themselves, and postulates and definitions are the bases of precepts or rules.[9] He characterized as grammatical arts the literary arts of history, arts of preparing texts and studying styles, which ignored the contents and the uses of history. He was convinced that the study of institutions and of republics must be based on the study of all peoples, not merely those of Western Europe, and in Chapter 6 "On the Constitution of Republics" (*De Statu Rerumpublicarum*), he criticizes the theory that the mixed constitution is the best, which was held by Polybius, Cicero, Machiavelli, Contarini, and Thomas More among others[10] and instead studies the kinds of constitutions and revolutions. Chapter 7 is devoted to the refutation of the theory of the four monarchies and the four golden centuries,[11] and the final and tenth chapter sets forth the order and collection of histories arranged according to time and subject matter, from Moses and the Book of Genesis to histories written in 1570; from Universal Histories through histories of particular peoples to histories of particular men.

The controversial oppositions concerning the art and method of history were drawn on issues concerning the use of the methods of literary history, of the history of law, and of the study of institutions and republics. The transition in the fourteenth century from the methods of Bartolus of Sassoferato to an appeal to literature and the history of law, which began in Petrarch, Boccaccio, and Salutati, took the form of a detailed attack on Bartolus in Lorenzo Valla's *Contra Bartolum Libellum cui Titulus de In-*

signis et Armis Epistola; in this controversy Bodin opposed Cujas and the grammarians, and he revised his view of Bartolus and practical men of law:

That was when I was lecturing publicly in Roman law at Toulouse, and amid the throng of young men I seemed very wise. I thought that those princes of legal science — that is, Bartolus, Baldus, Alexander, Faber, Paulus and Molinaeus, all outstanding figures — and virtually the whole order of judges and advocates knew nothing, or very little. But after I had been initiated into the mysteries of jurisprudence in the law courts, and had found corroboration through long experience in public affairs, then at last I understood that a real and solid knowledge of the law is found not in the dust of the schools, but in the battleground of the forum; not in the quantities of syllables, but in the scales of justice and equity. Those who know nothing of public affairs remain in the greatest ignorance of Roman law. . . . Thus I declare that of all those disciplines whose end relates to action, the one that least of all can do without practical experience is jurisprudence; and most of all at the present time, when the endless variety of laws and customs would overburden the tender minds of the young before they have learned to know what is useful.[12]

Bodin calls Machiavelli one of those who have profaned the sacred mysteries of political philosophy, and characterizes him as one who has been fashionable among the agents of tyrants,[13] yet the doctrines of Machiavelli and Bodin are associated in the criticism of Antonio Possevino.[14] Other Collections or "Storehouses" placed Bodin's *Method of History* and *Republic* in the context, not of the controversy of history and literature, nor of history, philology, literature, jurisprudence, and constitutions, but in the context of the long history of treatises on history. One such storehouse, the *Artis Historicae Penus* edited by Johannes Wolfius,[15] includes ancient as well as contemporary treatises, Lucian's treatise on how history should be written and Dionysius of Halicarnassus's judgment of Thucydides, as well as recent treatises on the nature, organization, and utility, the reading, writing, and teaching of history. Possevino refers to Bodin's work as *Methodus Historiae*, the title under which it appears in the *Artis Historicae Penus* is *Methodus Historica*. The "Storehouse" also contains Balduinus's conjunction of universal history with jurisprudence, *De Historia Universa et eius Conjunctione cum Jurisprudentia Prolegomenon*, which organizes history according to states, laws, public affairs, times, geography, cosmography; Christophorus Mylaeus's *De Scribenda Universitatis Rerum Historia Libri Quinque*, which divides history into five kinds according to its subject matter: the history of nature, of prudence, of principality (or society and community), of wisdom, and of literature; the dialogues on history of Patrizzi and Pontanus; Theodorus Zwingerus's *De Historia*, which lists the inventors and authors of history: ecclesiastical, universal, and particular histories, beginning with historians of the Jews and going through a long list to historians of the New World, and finally the writers of lives, divided into the lives of men and the lives of women; and Antononius Riccobonus's *De Historia Liber*, which, after a preliminary examination of the questions, What is history and what were the laws of history? (there are four laws of history), and How do the experts in the other arts aid history? — the grammarians, the poets (poetry is defined as the art of imitating the truth of history in fictive fables, a definition echoed by Francis Bacon), the orators, and the philosophers — presents the fragments of ancient Roman historians from Cato to Julius Hyginus.

From the controversies concerning the art and method of history in the sixteenth century developed all the lines of progress in the arts of history and of historical scholarship from the seventeenth to the nineteenth century, when new controversies arose, with echoes of the old, concerning the "methodology" of historiography, the humanities, and the sciences. In the seventeenth century Gerardus Joannes Vossius epitomized one line of the sixteenth-century controversies in his *Ars Historica, sive de Historiae et Historicae Natura Historiaeque Scribendae Praeceptis Commentatio,* in which he treats the nature of the art under the four rhetorical questions, whether history is, what it is, its external causes (its final causes or purposes and its efficient causes or the first writers of history), and its distribution (of histories into divine, natural, and human, and of the art of history into two parts, based on the subject matter and ends of history [things, that is, civil prudence and words] or into three parts [what we write, in what order, and with what words and sentences, that is, the comprehension of things, the disposition of things, and elocution or ornamentation]); his *De Historicis Graecis* in three books; and his *De Historicis Latinis* in three books. Vossius also wrote an *Epitome of Universal History* from Adam to 1600, a *De Studiorum Ratione Dissertatio Gemina, Generalis et Particularis* and an *Oratio de Historiae Utilitate,* as well as a series of systematic treatises on the liberal arts, on grammar, on rhetoric, on poetic, on the nature and constitution of the arts and sciences divided into five books, (1) on the four popular arts (grammatistic [that is, the science of reading and writing], gymnastic, music, and painting), (2) on philology, (3) on mathematics, (4) on logic, and (5) on philosophy, and a book on the sects of philosophers. The study of the history of historians, the edition of their works and their fragments, and the higher and lower criticism of their texts has gone apace since the time of G. J. Voss and Richard Bentley.

We have not only built on the foundations laid by the partisans of the philological interpretation of the art of history but we have followed the lead of each of the three proposed divisions of the substantive interpretations of the art of history. (1) We have adapted Mylaeus's fivefold division of history, in a restricted and literal form: we still talk about natural history but we tend to make it biological; we have reduced the history of prudence to a history of customs, cultures or mores, and myths; we have split universal history into particular histories of societies and communities, nations and regions, but we have multiplied them to include all the peoples of the world; we have transformed the history of wisdom into histories of philosophy and of the sciences; and we have made the history of literature into histories of literatures. (2) We have conformed to Bodin's judgment that it is wise to begin with human history rather than with natural history or divine history. That is the subject matter studied and taught in departments of history; the other forms of history in Mylaeus's classification are studied and taught in other departments of a modern university, and they are independent histories, adjusted to each other only by occasional and unintrusive exercises of interdepartmental cooperation, because the task of covering the history of all times and all places is already overwhelming for historians and departments of history without adding the problems of the history of all subject matters and of all that man has said, and made, and done.

(3) In conforming to Bodin's choice of human history, we have not followed his judgment of the subject matter of history as universal law and the republic; but although we have abandoned that universal subject matter in history, we have continued Bodin's inquiry, and we have discovered the subject matter of the social sciences. Montesquieu's *Spirit of the Laws* approaches the problem of constitutions on assumptions and by methods similar to Bodin's. "I have posited principles," Montesquieu writes in his *Préface*, "and I have seen that the particular cases comply to them as if by themselves, that the histories of all nations are only consequences to them, and that each law is bound to another law or depends on another more general law." Voltaire was among the numerous commentators on the *Spirit of the Laws* in the eighteenth century, and Destutt de Tracy's *Commentary* was first published in an English translation revised by Thomas Jefferson, prior to its publication in France and in French, early in the nineteenth century. Political science grew out of the study of the history of political institutions, economics out of the study of the wealth of nations, sociology out of the study of lesser and nonpolitical associations and communities, beginning with underprivileged or alienated groups, and anthropology out of the study of the customs and cultures of men, beginning with primitive and nonpolitical actions and institutions.

The conception of the liberal arts that took its beginning in the early Renaissance reached its culmination in the nineteenth century, when the vastly multiplied fields or "disciplines" and vastly variegated facts and data raised problems concerning the methodology proper to each field and the relations of the methodologies to each other. Controversies concerning whether the method of the natural sciences was the same or different from the method of the human or "spiritual" science, the humanities and the social sciences, reoriented our conception of the liberal arts and scientific methods. The method of the *Geisteswissenschaften* was identified with the method of history and with the study of concrete facts and values; and the sciences of spirit were transformed into the sciences of culture. The conception of the Renaissance as a historical period and a culture was developed as part of these nineteenth-century controversies, and the historical facts which constituted the culture of the Renaissance were discovered and ordered by use of the methods of the sciences of spirit. We have been busy since the end of the nineteenth century transforming the cultural sciences and the liberal arts. We have recognized the danger of fragmentation of knowledge when the arts and sciences are conceived as fields or subject matters as they have been increasingly since the Renaissance, and in the perspective of this reorientation of methods, we have reexamined our fixed scheme of the culture of the Renaissance and of the culture of the Middle Ages, drawn up in the orientation provided by the Renaissance conception of arts and methods. We have a problem of transforming the liberal arts and scientific methods once more, as the Renaissance transformed the medieval arts and sciences. We shall not make that transformation, or innovation, or rebirth by returning to the medieval conception of universal arts applicable to all subject matters or to the Renaissance conception of arts adapted to particular sets of facts and subject matters which can be universalized and applied to all knowledge and action, of a scientific method which will give content and precision to history and the humanities, or a humanistic method which will give generality and value to the sciences. It seems probable at this stage of our transformation that we shall have to find universal arts, comparable to the medieval arts, which will make interdisciplinary connections among the rich array of facts and values discovered and ordered by arts and methods, comparable to the Renaissance and early modern arts and methods. In this labor the history of arts, sciences, and institutions may make an important contribution by reexamining, from our present perspective, the liberal arts of the Middle Ages and the Renaissance, freed from the nineteenth-century perspective in which most of our prevalent views of the periods and of their accomplishments and values were constructed.

BY RICHARD MCKEON

NOTES

1. Ioannis Saresberienis, *Metalogicon*, ed. C. C. I. Webb (Oxford, 1929), Lib. IV, cap. 6 and 8, 170-71, 172.

2. Cf. R. McKeon, "Philosophy and the Development of Scientific Methods," *Journal of the History of Ideas*, XXVII (1966), 10-17.

3. D'Alembert, *Discours Preliminaire de l'Encyclopédie*, ed. F. Picavet (Paris, 1894), pp. 12-13.

4. W. H. Woodward, *Vittorino da Feltre and other Humanist Educations: Essays and Versions* (Cambridge, 1921), p. 106.

5. N. Machiavelli, *Discourses on the First ten Books of Titus Livius*, Bk. I, Introduction.

6. J. Bodin, *Methodus ad Facilem Historiarum Cognitionem, Oeuvres Philosophiques de Jean Bodin*, ed. Pierre Mesnard (Paris, 1951), p. 107.

7. Bodin, *Methodus*, p. 109.

8. Bodin, *Methodus, Caput Primum: Quid historia sit et Quotoplex*, p. 114.

9. Bodin, *Methodus*, p. 107. Cf. *Juris Universi Distributio, Oeuvres Philosophiques*, pp. 67-97.

10. Bodin, *Methodus*, pp. 177, 180.

11. Bodin, *Methodus*, pp. 223-28. Bodin connects the theory of the four monarchies with German historians — Luther, Melancthon, Sleidan, Funck, Lucidus, and Panvinio. The four empires listed in Melancthon's revision of the *Chronicon Carionis* are the Chaldean-Assyrian, the Persian, the Greco-Roman, and the German. The *Chronicon Carionis* is another universal history from the creation to the sixteenth century in five books and a supplement extending the narrative from 1519 to 1600.

12. Jean Bodin, *The Six Bookes of a Commonweale*, ed. K. D. McRae (Cambridge, Mass., 1962), second preface to the *République*, p. A 71.

13. Bodin, preface to the first edition of the *République*, p. A 69.

14. The Latin translation of the *Prince* was published in a single duodecimo volume with a series of attacks on Machiavelli, *Nicolai Machiavelli Florentini Princeps ex Sylvestri Telli Fulginatis traductione diligenter emendatus* (Leiden, 1643). The translation of the Prince occupies the first 117 pages, the writings against Machiavelli extend from p. 118 to p. 448. Possevino's *Judicium de Nicolai Machiavelli et Ioannis Bodini quibusdam Scriptis, quorum Catalogum haec pagina indicat* runs from p. 157 to p. 210; the catalogue includes the collection called *Antimachiavelli* (which is as pestiferous as the book of Machiavelli, p. 261) and the *Method of History*, the *Republic*, and the *Daemonomania* of Bodin.

15. *Artis Historicae Penus* (Basel, Petrus Perna, 1576). The first edition of Johannes Wolfius's "storehouse," which was published in 1567, contained twelve treatises; the second contained eighteen. They are listed in John L. Brown, *The Methodus ad Facilem Historiarum Cognitionem of Jean Bodin, a Critical Study* (Washington, D.C., 1939), p. 48. Thirteen of the eighteen treatises were

published by the same publisher in 1576 (the same year as the second edition of Wolfius's collection) under the title *Io. Bodini Methodus Historica, Duodecim eiusdem Argumenti Scriptorum, tam Veterum quam Recentiorum Commentariis Adaucta,* with a preface by the publisher, but without Wolfius's preface.

SELECTIVE BIBLIOGRAPHY
1. The Liberal Arts as Disciplines and as Subject Matters

Benetti-Brunelli, V. *Le Origini Italine della Scuola Umanistica.* Milan, 1919.

Crescini, A. *Le Origini del Metodo Analitico. Il Cinquecento.* Trieste, 1965.

McKeon, R. "Renaissance and Method in Philosophy," *Studies in the History of Ideas,* III (New York, 1952), 37-114.

———. "Introduction to the Philosophy of Cicero," Marcus Tullius Cicero, *Brutus, On the Nature of the Gods, On Divination, On Duties* (Chicago, 1950), pp. 1-65.

———. "Man and Mankind in the Development of Culture and the Humanities," in *Changing Perspectives on Man,* ed. B. Rothblatt (Chicago, 1968), pp. 283-94.

———. "Philosophy and the Development of Scientific Methods," *Journal of the History of Ideas,* XXVII (1966), 3-22.

———. "Poetry and Philosophy in the Twelfth Century," in *Critics and Criticism, Ancient and Modern,* ed. R. Crane (Chicago, 1952), pp. 297-318.

———. "Rhetoric in the Middle Ages," *Critics and Criticism,* pp. 260-96.

Siegel, J. E. *Rhetoric and Philosophy in Renaissance Humanism. The Union of Eloquence and Wisdom, Petrarch to Valla.* Princeton, N.J., 1968.

Vasoli, C. *La Dialettica e la Retorica dell'Umanesimo, "Invenzione" e "Metodo" nella Cultura del XV e XVI Secolo.* Milan, 1968.

Gruterus, I. *Lampas, sive Fax Artium Liberalium, hoc est, Thesaurus Criticus, quo Infinitis Locis Theologorum, Jurisconsultorum, Medicorum, Philosophorum, Oratorum, Historicorum, Poetarum, Grammaticorum, Scripta Supplentur, Corriguntur, Illustrantur, Notantur.* Frankfort, 1602. Four volumes, of 1,500 unnumbered pages each, containing detailed reports of texts, emendations, and variant readings.

Crenius, T., ed. *De Philologia, Studiis Liberalis Doctrinae, Informatione et Educatione Litteraria Generosorum Adolescentum, Compararanda Prudentia juxta et Eloquentia Civili, Libris et Scriptoribus ad eam Rem maxime Aptis, quoque Ordine Scriptorum Historiae Romanae Monumenta sint Legenda, Tractatus.* Leiden, 1696. Contains treatises by Budé, Campanella, Pastorius, Rosius, Scheffer, and Bargaeus on philology, the education of the young, rhetoric, and civil prudence (concerning the authors of histories and of the theory of social and moral sciences).

Crenius, T., ed, *Animadversiones Philologicae et Historicae, Novas Librorum Editiones, Praefationes, Indices, Nonnullasque Summorum aliquot Virorum Labeculas Notatas Excutientes.* Leiden, 1697.

—————. *De Eruditione Comparanda in Humanioribus, Vita, Studio Politico, Cognitione Auctorum Ecclesiasticorum, Historicorum, Politicorum ac Militarium, item Peregrinatione Tractatus.* Leiden, 1699. Contains treatises by Camerarius, Fungerus, Clapmarius, Colerus, Caselius, Hanniel, Aegidius a Lancken, Bosius, Naudaeius, Thomasonus, Ranzovius, Alsted, Berneggerus, Justus Lipsius, and Georgius Richter on the education of the young, including a three-year course of studies for the sons of nobles, the study of political science, and the relations of, and methods of treating, the arts and the sciences.

—————. *Consilia et Methodi Aureae Studiorum optime Institutendorum Praescripta Studiosae Juventutis a Maximis in Re Litteraria J. Fortio Ringelbergio, D. Erasmo Rotterodamo, etc. cuius Accedunt Opuscula de Cognitione sui.* Rotterdam, 1692.

Gerhard John Voss illustrates the way in which one tradition of the transformation of the liberal arts into subject matters was brought to an inclusive and learned culmination at the beginning of the eighteenth century. His *Opera*, published in six large folio volumes from 1695 to 1701, include:

Volume I, *Etymologicus*, which contains:

    1. *De Literarum Permutatione Tractatus,*

    2. *Etymologicon Linguae Latinae,* an etymological dictionary.

Volume II, *Philologicus*, which contains:

    1. *Aristarchus, sive de Arte Grammatica Libri Septem, quibus Censura in Grammaticos praecipue Veteres Exercetur, Causae Linguae Latinae eruuntur Scriptores Romani Illustrantur vel Emendantur.* Book I expounds the nature of the art of grammar in general and treats the letter; Book II goes on to the syllable; Books III to VI are four books *De Vocum Analogia et Anomalia* — Book III on the division, number, and case of nouns, Book IV on the declension of nouns, Book V on verbs, Book VI on the remaining six classes of words; Book VII is *De Sermonis Constructione.*

    2. *De Vitiis Sermonis et Glossematis Latino-Barbaris Libri Novem, partim Utiles ad Pure Loquendum, partim ad melius Intelligendos Posteriorum Saeculorum Scriptores.*

Volume III, *Philologicus*, which contains:

    1. *Commentariorum Rhetoricorum sive Oratoriarum Institutionum Libri sex.* Book I expounds the nature, parts and issues of rhetoric; Book II is on the passions; Book III on the parts of an oration; Book IV on periods and tropes; Book V on figures of speech and thought; Book VI on character and style.

    2. *De Rhetoricae Natura et Constitutione Liber.*

    3. *De Arte Poeticae Natura et Constitutione Liber.*

    4. *Poeticarum Institutionum Libri Tres.*

5. *De Imitatione, tum Oratoria, tum praecipue Poetica, deque Recitatione Veterum, Liber.*

6. *De Veterum Poetarum Temporibus Libri Duo.*

7. *De Artium et Scientiarum Natura ac Constitutione Libri Quinque, antehac diversis titulis editi.*

Lib. I. *De Quatuor Artibus Popularibus.* The four popular arts are grammatistic (reading and writing), gymnastic, music, and painting.

Lib. II. *De Philologia.* "Polymathy" or "encyclopedia," the cycle of the arts or the liberal arts are the arts which prepare for philosophy. Polymathy has three parts: philology (which is also called grammar), mathematics, and logic. Philology is divided into the formative arts of speech and history. The arts of speech are grammar (methodic and exegetic), rhetoric, and metric. History is divided into geography, chronography, genealogy, and pragmatic history or history properly speaking.

Lib. III. *De Mathesi.*

Lib. IV. *De Logica.* Three names are applied to this discipline — logic, dialectic, and critic (by the Stoics) — and possibly a fourth should be added — canonic (by the Epicureans).

Lib. V. *De Philosophia.*

8. *De Philosophorum Sectis Liber.*

Volume IV, *Historicus et Epistolicus*, which contains:

1. *Ars Historica sive de Historiae et Historices Natura Historiaeque Scribendae Praeceptis Commentatio.*

2. *De Historicis Graecis, Libri Quatuor.*

3. *De Historicis Latinis, Libri Tres.*

4. *Historiae Universalis Epitome.*

5. Various opuscules follow, among which is *De Studiorum Ratione Dissertatio Gemina, Generalis et Particularis.* The General Part is in two parts, (1) of what disciplines perfect erudition is composed, and (2) how the various disciplines are best learned; the Particular Part is *De Ratione et Ordine Universam Legendi Historiam.*

Volume V, *De Idolatria Gentili*, which contains: *De Theologia Gentili, et Physiologia Christiana; sive de Origine et Progressu Idolatriae; deque Naturae Mirandis, quibus Homo Adducitur ad Deum Libri Novem.*

Volume VI, *Theologicus*, which contains ten treatises, including: *Chronologiae Sacrae Isagoge, sive de Ultimis Mundi Antiquitatibus, ac inprimis de Temporibus Rerum Hebraearum Dissertationes Octo*, and several treatises on theological disputations and theological and historical theses.

Boecler, J. H. *Bibliographia Critica. Scriptores Omnium Artium atque Scientiarum Ordine Praecensens.* First edition 1677. Emended and enlarged by J. G. Krause, Leipzig, 1715.

Boecler distinguished two ways of treating all things that can be taught and learned — (1) according to the disciplines and (2) according to the things treated by the disciplines. Christophorus Mylaeus and John Sturm use the first method and G. J. Voss uses the second. Boecler follows Voss and divides the arts, sciences and disciplines into vulgar, popular, liberal, and philosophic arts. The four kinds of arts, and their subdivisions, are treated in sequence in the *Bibliography*.

The vulgar and popular arts are treated in Chapter 1. The vulgar or sordid arts, which are also called illiberal, vile, mercenary, and arts of the market-place, are the arts which contribute to the material basis of the community; they are the arts of the worker, the mechanic, the artisan. The popular arts are grammatistic (reading, writing, and printing), gymnastic, music, and painting.

The liberal arts are Philology, Mathematics, and Logic.

Philology is treated in Chapters 2 to 28.

Grammar is treated in Chapter 2: technical and exegetical grammar, Greek and Latin, and writers on grammar.

Rhetoric is treated in Chapter 3: rhetoricians, orators, and letter-writers.

Poesy is treated in Chapter 4: writers of poetics, poets, and critics.

History is treated in Chapters 5 to 27.

Histories of times or chronology, histories of places or geography, and histories of families or genealogy are treated in Chapter 5.

Histories of actions are divided into universal history (Chapter 6) and particular histories: ecclesiastical (Chapter 7) and civil — ancient (Jewish, Greek, Roman, and Byzantine, Chapters 8-11) and more recent (European histories, Chapters 12-22, Asian, Chapter 23, African and American, Chapter 24), literary, Chapter 25, and biographies, Chapter 26.

Chapter 27 is concerned with writers who are historians in the sense of treating "various things," such as Aelianus, *Varia Historia,* Valerius Maximus's *Facta et Dicta Memorabilia,* Peter Crinitius's *De Honestis Disciplinis et Poetis,* Raphael Maffei's (or Voterranus's) *Commentarii Urbani,* and the Elzevir Republics. (*The Commentarii Urbani* is a universal history and an inclusive encyclopedia of "various things" in three parts: *Geography,* in which cities and places are ordered according to countries, *Anthropology,* in which famous men of all times are treated in six ages, and *Philology,* in which the rudiments of the various arts and sciences are set forth, concluding with four chapters on the "cyclic sciences": grammar, oratory, the mathematical sciences, and optics and catoptrics.) Chapter 28 does a like task for the entire section on philology by treating philologists who do not fall under any one of the disciplines enumerated, such as Athenaeus, Lucian, Aulus Gellius, Apuleius, Macrobius, Martianus Capella, John of Salisbury, and a long list of Renaissance and early modern philologists.

Mathematics is treated in Chapters 29-38.

Pure mathematics (arithmetic and geometry) in Chapters 29-30; mixed mathematics (logistic, music, optics, geodesy, cosmography, divided into astronomy and mathematical geography, and mechanics, in Chapters 31-38. Writers on Logic are treated in Chapter 39.

Philosophy in general is the subject of Chapter 40. It is divided into theoretic (physics and metaphysics, Chapters 41-42) and practical (ethics, politics, and economics, Chapters 43-45). To these are added as related to philosophy, theology, jurisprudence, and medicine (Chapters 46-48).

2. The Encyclopedia or Cycle of the Arts and Sciences as Programs of Education, Projects of Discovery, and Organizations of Knowledge

Education and Erudition

Battaglia, F. *Il Pensiero Pedagogico del Rinascimento*. Florence, 1960.

Garin, E. *L'Educazione in Europa, 1400-1600*. Bari, 1957.

———. *Il Pensiero Pedagogico dell'Umanesimo*. Florence, 1958.

Saitta, G. *L'Educazione dell'Umanesimo in Italia*. Venice, 1928.

Vidari, G. *L'Educazione in Italia dell'Umanesimo al Rinascimento*. Rome, 1930.

Woodward, W. H. *Studies in Education during the Age of the Renaissance*. Cambridge, 1906.

———. *Vittorino da Feltre and other Humanist Educations: Essays and Versions*. Cambridge, 1921.

Treatises on the nature and organization of "studies" were frequent in the sixteenth century, and collections of them were edited in the seventeenth century. Treatises with that title by Erasmus and by Joachim Ringelberg were published separately in the sixteenth century and in a single volume in the seventeenth, as in the edition of Leiden, 1634. Ringelberg's treatise was the first item of several collections of his essays on the arts: *Lucubrationes vel potius κυκλοπαιδεια* in 1529, *Lucubrationes: nempe Liber de Ratione Studii, utriusque Linguae Grammaticae, Rhetoricae, Mathematicae et Sublimioris Philosophiae* in 1541, and *Opera, quae proxima pagina enumerantur* in 1531. The contents enumerated on the next page are ordered under headings – those that pertain to grammar, to dialectic, to rhetoric, to mathematics, to divination, and those common to any nature (three treatises – *Chaos, Experimenta,* and *Liber de Homine*). In its first appearance in a printed title, the word "cyclopedia" was applied to the cycle of knowledge in courses of study, not to collections of facts.

Vives, J. L. *De Ratione Studiis Epistolae Duae, quibus absolutissimam Ingenuorum Adolescentium ac Puellarum Institutionem Doctissima Brevitate Complectitur*. Paris, 1527.

———. *De Disciplinis Libri XX*. Antwerp, 1531. Contains twelve books, seven on the decay of learning and five on Christian education which were sometimes published separately under the title *De Disciplinis XII, septem de*

Corruptis Artibus; quinque de Tradendis Disciplinis, as in the edition of Leiden, 1636.

Grotii, H. et aliorum Dissertationes de Studiis Instituendis, Amsterdam, 1645, contains Erasmus's and Ringelberg's treatises among the twenty-four collected, as well as Gabriel Naudé's *Bibliographia Politica* and his *Syntagma de Studio Liberali,* Campanella's *De Libris Propriis, et recta Ratione Studendi, Syntagma,* Leonardus Aretinus's *De Studiis et Literis,* and Joannes Albertus Bannus's *De Musicae Natura, Origine, Progressu, et denique Studio bene Instituendo.*

Vossii, Gerardi Io. et aliorum Dissertationes De Studiis bene Instituendis, Utrecht, 1658, is a like collection of twenty-two treatises. It repeats some of the treatises of the Grotius volume, such as Bannus's treatise on music, but adds others such as Vossius's *Dissertatio Bipartita,* the first part of which treats the question, of what disciplines is perfect erudition constituted, and the second the question, how are the various disciplines best learned, Justus Lipsius's *De Ratione Legendi Historiam,* and Jacobus Acontius's *De Investigandarum Tradendarumque Artium ac Scientiarum Methodo.*

The organization of courses of study often took the form of literary and philosophic history as in:

Struve, Burcard Gotthelf. *Introductio in Notitiam Rei Litterariae et Usum Bibliothecarum. Accesit Dissertatio de Doctis Impostoribus, et huic Quartae Editioni Accedunt Supplementa Necessaria et Oratio de Meritis Germanorum in Historiam.* 4th ed. Jena, 1715 (1st ed. 1703). Struve distinguishes literary history from polymathy, encyclopedia, and pansophy. Literary history consists of knowledge of things (*notitia rerum*) which determine the constitution of the republic of letters. Polymathy is exercised in knowledge of a variety of things by knowledge of almost all the arts. Encyclopedia contains the complex of the liberal arts adapted to criticism in a variety of ways. Pansophy comprehends all the parts of philosophy (Cap. I, §§ V and VI, pp. 5-7). The *Introduction* proceeds from the study of books about collections of books or Libraries to the use of libraries to the study of writers and publishing houses in eleven chapters: (1) "De Historia Litteraria" on earlier "*bibliothecae,*" (2) on the history of past Libraries or collections of books, (3) on foreign Libraries, (4) on German Libraries, (5) on the use of libraries, (6) on learned ephemerides, (7) on the lives of writers, (8) on the judgment of writers, (9) on condemned and prohibited books, (10) on literary societies, (11) on publishers.

————. *Selecta Bibliotheca Historica.* Jena, 1705. The *Select Historical Library* went through several editions and was expanded by Johann Georg Meusel into the *Bibliotheca Historica,* 1782-1804, in 11 volumes.

Juncker, C. *Lineae Primae Eruditionis Universae et Historiae Philosophicae ac Speciatim earum Disciplinarum in quibus Necesse est atque Utile Instrui ac Praeparari Juvenes Studioso in Academiis et Gymnasiis Illustribus.* Altenburg, 1714.

Heumann, C. A. *Conspectus Reipublicae Literariae sive Via ad Historiam Literariam*

Iuventuti Studiosae Aperta. Göttingen, 1717.

Stoll, G. *Introductio in Historiam Litterariam in Gratiam Cultorum Elegantiorum Litterarum et Philosophiae Conscripta.* Jena, 1728.

Sometimes the orientation is to universal erudition.

Gesner, J. M. *Primae Lineae Isagoges in Eruditionem Universalem, nominatim Philologiam, Historiam, et Philosophiam in Usum Praelectionum Ducta.* Second enlarged edition. 2 vols. Leipzig, 1783-84.

Sometimes the orientation is to history, theology, and controversies.

Possevinus, Antonius. *Bibliotheca Selecta, qua agitur de Ratione Studiorum in Historia, in Disciplinis, in Salute Omnium Procuranda.* 2 vols. Rome, 1793. (First ed. Cologne, 1607, one folio volume). In 28 Chapters (1) on the Dignity of man and the bearing of studies on it, (2) on Divine History or Positive Theology, (3) on Scholastic Theology and Practical Theology or Casuistry, (4 and 5) on Catechetic Theology or education, (6) on Relations with the Greeks and the Aquitanians, those who follow the Greek ritual, (7) on the method of treating controversies with Heretics, (8) on the Theology and Atheisms of heretics (particularly Lutherans and Calvinists), (9) on the way to procure the Salvation of Jews, Mohammedans, and other peoples, (10 and 11) on ways to procure the salvation of Japanese and other Oriental peoples, Part II, Volume II, (12) Jurisprudence, (13) Philosophy, (14) Medicine, (15) Mathematics, (16) Human History, (17) Pagan, Human, and Fabulous Poetry and Painting, compared with True and Sacred, and (18) Cicero compared with pagan and sacred writers with respect to the art of writing letters and the art of speaking, including ecclesiastical rhetoric.

———. *Apparatus ad Omnium Gentium Historiam. Expenditur Historici Graeci, Latini, et alii.* Venice, 1597.

———. *Apparatus Sacer ad Scriptores Veteris et Novi Testamenti, eorum Interpretes, Synodos et Patres Latinos ac Graecos, horum Versiones, Theologos Scholasticos quicumque contra Hereticos egerunt, chronographos et Historiographos Ecclesiasticos.* Cologne, 1608.

The Combinatory Art

Lully, Raymund. *Ars Magna, Generalis et Ultima.* Frankfort, 1596. In the tenth of the thirteen parts of the *Ars Magna*, "On Application," the other arts to which the great art is applicable are enumerated, among other applications, theology, philosophy, geometry, astronomy, arithmetic, music, rhetoric, logic, grammar, morals, politics, and law (pp. 361-82).

———. *Opera ea quae ad Inventam ab ipso Artem Universalem, Scientiarum Artiumque Omnium Brevi Compendio, Firmaque Memoria Apprehendarum, Locupletissimaque vel Oratione ex Tempore Pertractandarum, Pertinent.* Strasbourg, 1651.

The *Opera* contains six of Lully's works and five commentaries on his works, and one collection of selections from his works.

1. *Ars Brevis.*
2. *De Auditu Kabbalistico seu Kaballa.*
3. *Duodecim Principia Philosophiae Lullianae.*
4. *Dialectica seu Logica.*
5. *Rhetorica.*
6. *Ars Magna.*
7. Jordanus Brunus. *De Specierum Scrutinio.*
8. Idem. *De Lampade combinatoria Lulliana.*
9. Idem. *De Progressu et Lampade Venatoria Logicorum.*
10. Henricus Cornelius Agrippa. *Commentaria in Artem Brevem Raymundi Lullii.*
11. Raymond Lully. *De Articulis Fidei.*
12. Valerius de Valeriis. *Opus Aureum tam in Arborem Scientiarum quam Artem Generalem.*

Alsted, John Henry. *Clavis Artis Lullianae et Verae Logices.* Strasbourg, 1652.

Kircher, Athanasius. *Ars Magna Sciendi, in XII Libros Digesta, qua Nove et Universali Methodo per Artifiosum Combinationum Contextum de Omni Re Proposita Plurimis et prope Infinitis Rationibus Disputari, Omniumque Summaria quaedam Cognitio Comparari Potest.* Amsterdam, 1669.

On the engraved title page, the title is *Ars Magna Sciendi sive Combinatoria, quâ ad Omnium Artium Scientiarumque Cognitionem Brevi Adquirendam, Amplissima Porta Recluditur, quod uti Inventum Novum, ita quoque ejusdem Subsidio usque Instructus, quilibet de quavis Re Propostia, Infinitis paenè Rationibus Disputare, Omniumque Summarium quandam cujuslibet Doctrinae Notitiam Obtinere Poterit.*

The Table of Contents is followed by an enumeration of the arts and sciences to which the great art applies: "Paradigmata Scientiarum quibus Arts Nostra applicatur. 1. Theologiae Scholasticae, 2. Theologiae Positivae, 3. Theologiae Moralis, 4. Theologicae Ascesticae, 5. Controversiarum, 6. Metaphysicae, 7. Physicae, 8. Medicinae, 9. Logicae sive Dialecticae, 10. Juris Civilis, 11. Juris Canonis, 12. Politicae, 13. Ethicae, 14. Mathematicae, 15. Rhetoricae sive Humanarum Litterarum, quibus Universae Encyclopaediae ambitus absolvitur."

The *Ars Magna Sciendi* is in two volumes. In the first the elements and principles are set forth, the canons and precepts are laid down, and the method and scope of the art are presented in "paradigmata." In the second the rules and canons are applied to all the arts and sciences in examples and paradigms of questions. Book V, the final book of Volume I, on the division of the sciences and scientific principles is divided into two parts, the first concerned with the sciences and the modes of acquiring them, set forth in detailed paradigms of the seven classes of science — theology, metaphysics, physics, medicine, mathematics, moral philosophy, and the verbal sciences; the second concerned with the analytico-synthetic art or the composition and resolution of things, set forth in detailed paradigms. The six books of

Volume II present paradigms of the art constructed from related arts, sciences, and faculties or powers. Thus, Book VII is concerned with questions proper to metaphysics, logic or dialectic, physics, and medicine, and Book IX with the ascetic faculty, controversies of faith, and rhetoric. In Section I of Book IX, the ascetic faculty is identified as a supernatural practical habit ordered to the achievement of the final end, and related to scholastic theology as logic is related to metaphysics; it is often called "prudence," "wisdom," or the loftiest science. Section II treats of the use of the art to resolve controversies of faith, and Section III goes on to questions of rhetoric, the art of speaking aptly, distinctly, and ornately. In this context the related questions of rhetoric are considered relative to ends and contents rather than as persuasion by verbal and metal figures: Demonstrative Rhetoric is concerned with goods of the soul and goods of the body, with the diffusion of goods in the state, and with the satisfaction of needs and wants; Deliberative Rhetoric is concerned with the establishment of peace and security; Judicial Rhetoric is concerned with sanctions to preserve civil laws and constitutions, justice and piety. The illiberal or mechanical arts are necessary to the maintenance of the life of the individual and the community: they include agriculture, glassblowing, plastics, encaustics, mining, cooking, and innumerable others.

Leibniz, G. W. *Dissertatio de Arte Combinatoria, in qua ex Arithmeticae Fundamentis Complicationum ac Transpositionum Doctrina Novis Praeceptis Extruitur, et Usus Ambarum per Universum Scientiarum Orbem Ostenditur; Nova etiam Artis Meditandi seu Logicae Inventionis Semina Sparguntur.* Leipzig, 1666. (*Die Philosophischen Schriften von Gottfried Wilhelm Leibniz,* ed. C. J. Gebhardt. Berlin 1770, vol. IV, pp. 27-104.) Leibniz refers to Lully and Kircher.

Wilkins, John. *An Essay towards a Real Character and a Philosophical Language.* London, 1668. The *Essay* consists of four parts. The first is concerned with languages; the second contains "a regular enumeration and description of all those things and notions to which names are to be assigned"; the third contains a philosophical or "natural" grammar; and the fourth contains a real character and a philosophical language. The appendix is "An Alphabetical Dictionary, wherein all English Words according to their significations, are either referred to their Places in the Philosophical Tables, or explained by such words as are in those Tables."

Method and the Art of Discovery

Gilbert, N. W. *Renaissance Concepts of Method.* New York, 1960.

Callot, E. *La Renaissance des Sciences de la Vie an XVI Siècle.* Paris, 1951.

Agricola, Rudolph. *De Inventione Dialectica Libri Tres, cum Scholiis Joannis Matthei Phrissemii.* Cologne, 1538.

Peter Ramus proposed radical reorientations and changes in the liberal arts and the organization and methods of the sciences. He criticized the ancient writers on the arts and was the center of wide and violent controversies. His followers, the Ramists, recognized the revolutionary tendency of their method by calling themselves "Neoterics" or Moderns, much as the terministic logicians of the thirteenth and fourteenth centuries had called themselves "Moderni" or Moderns. The Neoterics determined the organization and methods of early American education in philosophy and theology at Harvard, Yale, and King's College (Columbia). A comprehensive inventory of his works is contained in:

> Ong, W. J., S.J. *Ramus and Talon Inventory: A Short-Title Inventory of the Published Works of Peter Ramus (1515-1572) and of Omer Talon (ca. 1510-1562) in their Original and their variously Altered Forms. With Related Material: 1. The Ramist Controversies: A Descriptive Catalogue. 2. Agricola Check List: A Short-Title Inventory of some Printed Editions and Printed Compendia of Rudolph Agricola's Dialectical Invention (De Inventione Dialectica).* Cambridge, Mass., 1958.

Father Ong takes a critical view of Ramus's influence in: *Ramus. Method, and Decay of Dialogue.* Cambridge, Mass., 1958.

> Digby, Everard. *Admonitioni F. Mildapetti Navareni de unica P. Rami Methodo Retinenda Responsio.* London, 1580.
>
> ———. *De Duplici Methodo, unicam P. Rami Methodum Refutantes, in quibus Via Plana, Expedita, et Exacta, secundum Optimos Autores ad Scientiarum Cognitionem Elucidatur.* London, 1580.
>
> ———. *Theoria Analytica, Viam ad Monarchium scientiarum Demonstrans, totius Philosophiae et Reliquarum Scientiarum, necnon Primorum Postremorum mysteria Arcanaque Dogmata Enucleans.* London, 1579.
>
> Case, John. *Summa Veterum Interpretum in Universam Dialecticam. Aristotelis, quam vere falsove Ramus in Aristotelem Invehatur, Ostendens.* London, 1584.
>
> Milton, John. *Artis Logicae plenior Institutio ad Petri Rami Methodum Concinnata.* London, 1672.

Francis Bacon criticizes the single methods of Lully and Ramus in: Bacon, Francis. *Of the Proficience and Advancement of Learning Human and Divine,* Bk. II (The Works of Francis Bacon, ed. J. Spedding, R. L. Ellis, and D. D. Heath, vol. III, pp. 403-9) London, 1857 and in *De Augmentis Scientiarum* VI, 2 (vol. V, pp. 448-54), but traces of the influence of both and approval of aspects of their methods may be found in his *Novum Organum.*

Dictionaries of Words and of Things and Organizations of Knowledge

Nizolius, Marius. *Observationes in M. T. Ciceronem.* Basel, 1520. A Latin Lexicon based on Cicero; nearly seventy printings between 1520 and 1630. The Basel 1548 edition appeared under the title *Nizolius sive Thesaurus Ciceronianus,* "Nizolius" and "Ciceronian Lexicon" having become synonymous terms.

———. *De Veris Principiis et de Vera Ratione Philosophandi contra Pseudophilosophos*

Libri IV, in quibus Statuuntur ferme omnia Vera Verarum Artium et Scientiarum Principia, Refutatis et Reiectis Prope Omnibus Dialecticorum et Metaphysicorum Principiis Falsis: et Praeterea Refelluntur fere omnes Marci Antonii Objectiones contra Ejusdem Nizolium, usque in hunc Diem Editae. Parma, 1553.

Leibniz edited Nizolius's work in two printings under two titles:

De Veris Principiis et Vera Ratione Philosophandi contra Pseudophilosophos, Libri IV. Frankfort, 1670, and *Anti-barbarus Philosophicus, sive Philosophia Scholasticorum Impugnata, Libris IV. De Veris Principiis et Vera Ratione Philosophandi contra Pseudophilosophos.* Frankfort, 1674.

A modern edition was published by Quirinus Breen (2 vols.), Rome, 1956.

According to Nizolius, "the first general principle of truth and of philosophizing rightly . . . is knowledge of and learning in the Greek and Latin languages in which almost everything that is most worthy to be known and thought, especially those things which pertain to the discipline of philosophy, particularly the Aristotelian philosophy, have been recorded and written" (Book I, Chap. I, p. 22). "The second general principle of truth is knowledge of the precepts and documents which are recorded in the Grammarians and the Rhetoricians. The precepts and traditions of the Grammarians and the Rhetoricians are truer and much more useful and necessary in investigating truths and philosophizing rightly than those of the dialecticians and metaphysicians." Nizolius proposes to dispute against "the dialecticians, metaphysicians, and all the other philosophasters instructed in and armed with no other precepts for speaking, or dividing, or defining, or arguing than those which he has learned from the Grammarians and Rhetoricians, or which he has discovered by himself or by reading proved authors" (ibid., p. 23). "The third general principle of truth is extended and assiduous reading of certain well proved authors, Greek and Latin, and understanding the common usage of speaking of those authors and of the people, 'which establishes the judgment, the law, and the norm of speaking,' as Horatius says most correctly in the *Ars Poetica* I. 72" (ibid., p. 26). "The fourth general principle of truth is the freedom and true license of perceiving and judging concerning all things, as truth itself and the nature of things demands . . . unrestrained by the dogmas of any philosophical sect" (ibid., pp. 26-27). The fifth and last general principle of truth is a complex of rules to avoid obscurity and unintelligibility, incoherence, and paradoxes (ibid., p. 28). Rhetoric becomes the truly universal or general art, grammar the first under it, and all the other arts and sciences are ordered under them. The subject matter of rhetoric is all the things in the world. The precepts of history, morals, politics, physics, mathematics are specifications of the precepts of rhetoric to the proper mode of speech on those subjects, and with respect to subject matter, all the things in the world are divided into four parts, the Demonstrative genus, or good and evil (*honestas vel turpitudo*), the Deliberative genus, or utility and inutility (*utilitas vel inutilitas*), the Judicial genus, or equity and inequity, and the

Philosophic genus, or truth and falsity.

Alstedt, Johan Heinrich. *Encyclopaedia Septem Tomis Distincta, I. Precognita Disciplinarum, Libris Quatuor* [1. Hexilogia, 2. Technologia, 3. Archelogia, 4. Didactica], *II. Philologia, Libris Sex* [1. Lexica, 2. Grammatica, 3. Rhetorica, 4. Logica, 5. Oratoria, 6. Poetica], *III. Philosophia Theoretica, Libris Decem* [1. Metaphysica, 2. Pneumatica, 3. Physica, 4. Arithmetica, 5. Geometria, 6. Cosmographia, 7. Uranometria, 8. Geographia, 9. Optica, 10. Musica], *IV. Philosophia Practica, Libris Quatuor* [1. Ethics, 2. Oeconomica, 3. Politica, 4. Scholastica], *V. Tres Superiores Facultates, Libris Tribus* [1. Theologia, 2. Jurisprudentia, 3. Medicina], *VI. Artes Mechanicae, Libris Tribus* [1. Artes Mechanicae in Genere, 2. Artes Mechanicae Mathematicae, 3. Artes Mechanicae Physicae], *VII. Farragines Disciplinarum, Libris Quinque* [1. Mnemonica, 2. Historica, 3. Chronologia, 4. Architectonica, 5. Quodlibetica]. 2 vols. Herborn, 1630.

Leibniz, G. W. *De Ratione Perficiendi Encyclopaediam Alstedii. Philosophische Schriften.* Berlin, 1966, vol. II, pp. 394-97.

Leibniz proposes as parts of an encyclopedia "Theoremata, Historiae, Observationes, Hypotheses, Problemata."

Ramus and Lully influenced the organization of Alstedt's *Encyclopaedia;* Francis Bacon provided the organization of the arts and sciences followed by the French *Encyclopédie.* For the transition from ancient to Renaissance and modern encyclopedias see R. McKeon, "Encyclopaedia," in *Encyclopaedia Britannica* (1968), vol. 8, pp. 363-69.

3. The Liberal Arts in Biographies and Bibliographies: from Lives of Illustrious Men and Ecclesiastical Writers to Ecclesiastical Libraries and Libraries of the Departments of Literature and Science and the Nations of Men

Taylor, Archer. *Renaissance Guides to Books. An Inventory and Some Conclusions.* Berkeley, California, 1945.

———. *A History of Bibliographies of Bibliographies.* New Brunswick, N.J., 1955.

———. *General Subject Indexes since 1548.* Philadelphia, Pa., 1966.

A comprehensive collection of the *Lives of Illustrious Men* and of *Ecclesiastical Writers* was published in:

Fabricius, John Albert. *Bibliotheca Ecclesiastica, in qua Continentur de Scriptoribus Ecclessiasticis S. Hieronymus cum . . . integris Erasmi, Mariani Victorii, Henr.*

Gravii, Aub. Miraei, Wilh. Ernesti Tentelii et Ern. Salomonis Cypriani Annotationibus, . . . Gennadius Massiliensis, . . . S. Isidorus Hispanalensis, Ildefonsus Toletanus, Honorius Augustodunensis, Sigebertus Gemblacensis, . . . Henricus Gandavensis, Anonymus Mellicensis, . . . Petrus Casinensis, de Viris Illustribus Monasterii Casinensis, . . . Jo. Trithemii Abbatis Spanhemensis, Liber de S. E., . . . Aub. Miraei, Auctarium de S. E., et a Tempore, quo desinit Trithemius, de Scriptoribus Saeculi XVI et XVII, Libri Duo. Hamburg, 1715.

Jerome's *De Viris Illustribus* (A.D. 392) is based on pagan antecedents in the *De Viris Illustribus* of Cornelius Nepos and Suetonius as well as on Eusebius. It contains 135 lives, ending with the life of Jerome himself.

Gennadius's *De Viris Illustribus* (ca. 480) opens with a prefatory life of Jerome and adds 100 later biographies. The last chapters (92-100) are probably by a later hand. The last is a life of Gennadius.

Isidore of Seville's *De Scriptoribus Ecclesiasticis* (616-18) contains 45 lives, of which the first 12 are probably by an earlier author.

Ildefonsus's *De Scriptoribus Ecclesiasticis* (ca. 607-69) adds 14 biographies from Gregory the Great to Pope Eugenius I. It is usually followed by several appendices which contain a life of Ildefonsus by Julian Archbishop of Toledo.

Sigebert of Gembloux's *De Scriptoribus Ecclesiasticis* (eleventh century) contains 171 biographies, repeating some of the lives in earlier collections and ending with a life of Sigebert, in which he describes his work as an imitation and completion of the Lives of Jerome and Gennadius.

Honorius of Autun's *De Scriptoribus* (twelfth century) is in four parts: (1) excerpted from Jerome (136 lives), (2) from Gennadius (97 lives), (3) from Isidore (40 lives), (4) from various authors (17 lives); 24 biographies are added to the lists of his three named predecessors.

Henry of Ghent (thirteenth century) treats 60 writers, mostly from the twelfth and thirteenth centuries.

John Tritheim's *De Scriptoribus Ecclesiasticis* (Basel, 1494) treats 963 entries. The biographical detail is greater and the bibliographical information more precise. In successive editions later authors were added to bring the list up to date; thus, in the edition of Cologna, 1546, Tritheim's work occupies 404 pages, and two sets of additions run from page 404 to page 494.

Aubertus Miraeus's (Aubert Le Mire) *Auctarium de Scriptoribus Ecclesiasticis, quorum Opera ex tot vel pro parte apud Veteres Nomenclatores Sacros, Hieronymum, Gennadium, Isidorum, Ildefonsum, Honorium, Sigebertum et Henricum Gandavensem Desiderantur,* was first published in 1638 under the title *Bibliotheca Ecclesiastica sive de Scriptoribus Ecclesiasticis Septem.* . . . In 1649 a second part was published posthumously, covering the writers from the time of John Tritheim to "our times." The materials from the writers up to Tritheim yield 554 lives. The writers of the sixteenth and seventeenth centuries (1494-1641) are set forth in more than 1600 brief biographies. There are two indexes, one of prenomina, the other of cognomina.

Bellarmine, Robert. *De Scriptoribus Ecclesiasticis Liber Unus. Cum adiunctis Indicibus XI et Brevi Chronologia ab Orbe Condito unque ad annum MDCXII.* Rome, 1613.

Bellarmine's work went through many successive editions in the seventeenth century, the first two revised by the author. The sequence of editions is a reflection and report of the growing body of Ecclesiastical Libraries. The 1613 edition is a book of 258 pages. The edition published in Paris in 1658 was edited by Philip Labbé with a philological and chronological appendix by the editor. It is still a handy little volume of 573 pages. The authors from Moses to the sixteenth century are covered in 427 octavo pages. There are about 550 lives (or, since Bellarmine has made the transition from biography to bibliography, about 2,500 titles) arranged by centuries. In the 1658 edition there are ten indexes in which the authors are classified under the headings: interpreters of Scripture, writers against heretics, scholastic theologians, canon lawyers, casuists, Christian orators, sacred poets, ecclesiastical historians, chronologists, and writers of books of piety, and a brief chronological table in two parts, from creation to Christ and from the birth of Christ to the year 1612. In addition to the ten indexes at the end, the eleventh, an alphabetical index of writers, is placed at the beginning of the book.

Labbé published *De Scriptoribus Ecclesiasticis, quos Attigit . . . Robertus Bellarminus, Philologica et Historica Dissertatio,* Paris, 1660, in two volumes of 2,000 pages.

André de Saussay published *Insignis Libri de Scriptoribus Ecclesiasticis, Eminentissimi Cardinalis Bellarmini Continuatio, ab Anno 1500, in quo Desinit, ad Annum 1660,* in Cologne in 1684.

Casimir Oudin's *Supplementum de Scriptoribus vel Scriptis Ecclesiasticis a Bellarmino Ommissis, ad annum 1460, vel ad Artem Typographicam Inventam* (Paris, 1686) contains 720 pages of additional information — among the writers added are Origen, Benedict, Peter Abailard, William of Ockham, and Raymond Sebond. It has four indexes and, at the end, a list of women ecclesiastical writers (six entries). This work was enlarged and issued in three volumes of almost 6,500 columns in 1722 under the title *Commentarius de Scriptoribus Ecclesiasticis Antiquis, tam Impressis quam Manuscriptis, adhuc extantibus in Celebrioribus Europae Bibliothecis, a Bellarmino, Possevino, Philippo Labbeo, Guilelmo Caveo, Ludovico Ellis Du Pin et aliis Omissis, ad Annum MCCCCLX, vel ad Artem Typographicam Inventam.*

For Antonio Possevino's *Apparatus Sacer* see Section II above, among his works *De Rationibus Studiorum.*

Cave, William. *Chartophylas Ecclesiasticus: prope MD. Scriptores Ecclesiastici, tam Minores, quam Majores, tum Catholici, tum Haeretici, eorumque Patria, Ordo, Secta, Munera, Aetas et Obitus; Opuscula, quin et ipsa Fragmenta breviter indicantur. Scriptores Dubii a Certis, Supposititii a Genuinis, Non-extantes a Superstitibus Distinguuntur. A Christo Nato ad Annum usque MDVII. Accedunt Gentiles*

Christiane Religionis Oppugnatores; et Brevis cujusvis Saeculi Conspectus. London, 1685. Three years later, Cave reviews the development of his work in the *Prolegomena* of his *Scriptorum Ecclesiasticorum Historia Literaria* (Sect. III, *De hujusce Operis Ortu et Progressu*). He estimates that the *Chartophylas* treats about 1,500 writers, but since it was too short and unpolished (*opusculum illud breve nimis et jejunum*), he wrote, yielding to the insistence of friends, a longer work and cast it in the form of a Literary History after so many *Libraries, Catalogues, Nomenclators,* and *Tables.* He notes that Du Pin and Oudin published their two works in 1686, the year after the *Chartophylas,* and he refers to Sextus Senensis, Posseviunus, Bellarmine, Miraeus, Labbeus, Gesner, Simler, Perkins, Scultetus, and Voss.

Cave, William. *Scriptorum Ecclesiasticorum Historia Literaria, a Christo nato usque ad Saeculum XIV Facili Methodo Digesta, qua de Vita illorum ac Rebus Gestis, de Secta, Dogmatibus, Elogio, Stylo; de Scriptis Genuinis, Dubiis, Suppositis, Ineditis, Deperditis, Fragmentis; deque Variis Operum Editionibus perspicue Agitur. Accedunt Scriptores Gentiles, Christianae Religionis Oppugnatores; et cujusvis Saeculi Breviarium.* . . . London, 1688-98 in two folio volumes. It contains two appendices "by other hands," Henry Wharton and Robert Gery, bringing the account from the year 1300 to 1517. At least six editions of Cave's work appeared in fifty years; the last (Basel, 1741-45) is in two large folio volumes of 1479 double-columned pages.

Both the *Chartophylas* and the *Historia Literaris* are divided into sixteen sections or books, one for each of the sixteen centuries, each characterized in the title, usually from the dominant heresy. The first century is *Saeculum Apostolicum,* the second *Saeculum Gnosticum,* the third *Saeculum Novatianum,* the fourth *Saeculum Arianum,* the twelfth *Saeculum Waldense,* the thirteenth *Saeculum Scholasticum,* the sixteenth *Saeculum Reformatum.* The differences of the Reformation are reflected in these collections: Bellarmine and Labbé were Jesuits, Oudin and Cave were protestants. The judgment of Morhof, himself a protestant, is stated in a footnote to his *Polyhistor, Literarium, Philosophicum, et Practicum,* that "we" can the more easily dispense. . . his continuator Henry Wharton. (The *Polyhistor* was published in part in Morhof's lifetime: Tomes I and II in 1688, and the first three books of Tome III in 1692. The remaining four chapters of Tome III, including the footnote, were published for the first time posthumously in the first complete edition, Lubeck, 1708, Tome III, Book IV, Paragraph 17, Johannis Molleri, *Hypomnemata Historico-Critico-Philologica,* p. 123.)

Du Pin, L. Ellies. *Nouvelle Bibliothèque des Auteurs Ecclesiastiques, Contenant de leur Vie, et le Catalogue, la Critique, et la Chronologie de leurs Ouvrages; le Sommaire de ce qu'ils Contiennent: un Judgement sur leur Style, et sur leur Doctrine, et le Denombrement des Differents Editions.* This was published in Paris in 1686. It appeared in a Latin translation in three folio volumes in 1692 and later in English translation. The third French edition (1693) is in 19 quarto volumes of from 300 to 400 double-columned pages.

4. The Liberal Arts as the Methods of History and as the Subject Matter of History and of Culture

Bodin, Jean. *Methodus ad facilem historiarum cognitionem*. Paris, 1566. In 1576, the *Methodus* was published with twelve other treatises on history under the title *Io. Bodini Methodus Historica, duodecim eiusdem argumenti Scriptorum, tam veterum quam recentiorum, Commentariis adaucta: quorum elenchum Praefationi subiecimus*. Basel, 1576. A second edition was issued in 1579 in two volumes and containing five additional treatises under the title *Artis Historicae Penus*. The eighteen treatises are the following (the five added in the 1576 edition are marked by an asterisk):

1. Ioan. Bodini Andegavensis *Methodus Historica*.
2. Fr. Patritii Dialogi x. *De Historia*.
3. Ioan. Pontanus *De Historia*.
4. Fr. Balduinus *De Historia Universa et eius cum Jurisprudentia Conjunctione* lib. 2.
5. Sebastiani Foxii-Morzilli *De Historica Institutione*.
6. Ioan. Anto. Viperanus *De Scribenda Historia*.
7. Fr. Robertellus *De Historia*.
8. Dionysius Halicarnasseus *De Thucydidis Historia Iudicium, cum Ducitii Praefatione*.
9. Christophorus Mylaeus *De Scribenda universitatis Rerum Historia libri quinque*.* The five books treat (1) the history of nature, (2) of prudence, (3) of principality, (4) of wisdom, and (5) of literature.
10. Ubertus Folietta *De Ratione Scribendae Historiae, and de Similitudine Normae Polybianae*.
11. Davis Chytraeus *De Lectione Historiarum recte Instituenda*.
12. Lucianus Samosatensis *De Scribenda Historia*.
13. Simon Grinaeus *De Utilitate Legendae Historiae*.
14. Caelius Secundus *De Historia Legenda Sententia*.
15. Christophorus Pezelius *Oratio de Argumento Historiarum, et Fructu ex earum Lectione Petendo*.*
16. Theodorus Zwingerus *De Historia*.*
17. Ioan. Sambucus *De Historia in Praefatione ad Bonfinii Historiam Ungariae*.*
18. Antonius Riccobonus *De Historia*.*

Chytraeus has a separate section *De Germanicarum Rerum et Ecclesiasticis Scriptoribus*, and detailed analyses of the arguments of the histories of Herodotus and Thucydides.

Zwinger presents a series of tables of Inventors of history, Ecclesiastical Historians, Universal Historians, Historians of particular peoples arranged according to nation, and lives of writers, first men, then women.

223

Developments in the Early Renaissance

Twenty-five hundred copies of this book
were published by
State University of New York Press,
Albany, New York,
in May 1972.

Design and calligraphy by Freeman Craw.

Set in Monotype Centaur and Arrighi (Series 252)
by Wolf Composition Company, Incorporated,
Reading, Massachusetts.
Initials are constructed square capitals
from Pacioli, *De Divina Proportione* (Venice, 1509).
Printed by offset lithography
on Mohawk Superfine Text,
and bound in Kennett book cloth
with lining papers of Fabriano Cover, 118,
by Edwards Brothers, Incorporated,
Ann Arbor, Michigan.